TALKS TO BOYS

Talks to Boys

Classic Teachings on
Virtues & Values

ELEANOR A. HUNTER

BRINGING TRUTH TO LIFE
NavPress Publishing Group
P.O. Box 35001, Colorado Springs, Colorado 80935

The Navigators is an international Christian organiza-
tion. Our mission is to reach, disciple, and equip
people to know Christ and to make Him known
through successive generations. We envision multi-
tudes of diverse people in the United States and every
other nation who have a passionate love for Christ,
live a lifestyle of sharing Christ's love, and multiply
spiritual laborers among those without Christ.

NavPress is the publishing ministry of The Navigators. NavPress publications help believers learn bibli-
cal truth and apply what they learn to their lives and
ministries. Our mission is to stimulate spiritual formation among our readers.

Library of Congress Catalog Card Number: 96-70635
ISBN 08910-99875

(Originally published as *Talks to Boys* by E. A.
Hunter, © copyright 1890 American Tract Society,
New York. This edition by permission.)

Cover illustration: Wood River Gallery

All Scripture quotations in this publication are taken
from the *King James Version* (KJV).

Printed in the United States of America

1 2 3 4 5 6 7 8 9 10 11 12 13 14 15 / 00 99 98 97 96

FOR A FREE CATALOG OF
NAVPRESS BOOKS & BIBLE STUDIES,
CALL 1-800-366-7788 (USA)
or 1-416-499-4615 (CANADA)

Contents

Preface

While circumstances and society have changed significantly within the past 100 years, right and wrong remain the same. But in a society where many no longer recognize the value of truth, honesty, and living upright and godly lives, it can be difficult to teach our children their necessity.

Originally published in 1890, *Talks to Boys* gives you a unique tool for teaching your children classic virtues and values. Each short essay on a different subject gives you a glimpse into the past, while teaching a timeless lesson suitable for any age.

Whether you read each chapter aloud as a family or encourage your children to read them alone, you'll be delighted with these charming lessons and stories from the past.

Questions for discussion have been added to the end of every chapter, giving you the opportunity to discuss each topic as a family. Few changes have been made to the text itself, with the exception of footnotes added to clarify the author's intention and selected words changed where necessary.

◦═◉═◦

Talks to Boys was originally published by the American Tract Society. Founded in 1825, the American Tract Society was at one time the largest publisher of both Christian and secular titles in the world. During the 1800s and early 1900s, the society published works by many well-known authors and theologians, including John Bunyan and Jonathan Edwards. The American Tract Society also published biographies, devotionals, reference works, books of theology, and children's books.

In the 1940s, they stopped publishing books and focused exclusively on tracts (pocket-sized pamphlets). Most of their current tracts emphasize evangelism for all occasions on a variety of contemporary subjects and social issues. American Tract Society is one of the largest producers of gospel tracts in the world today, publishing between twenty to thirty million each year. A free full-color tract catalog is available by calling (800)54-TRACT or (972)276-9408. For further information about the background and current ministry of the American Tract Society write P.O. Box 462008, Garland, TX 75046 or visit their web site at http://www.goshen.net/AmericanTractSociety

NavPress and the American Tract Society have an exclusive publishing relationship, in which NavPress will republish selected works from the American Tract Society book archives that address classic spirituality, family, and Puritan theology.

Trifles

They were only some little snowflakes,
So feathery, soft, and light;
Yet a host of them together
Stopped a train of cars one night;

<hr>

And the shivering, frightened people
Fought with hunger and cold
Long hours ere they were rescued
From the little snowflakes' hold.

<hr>

They were only some little raindrops
Who lived afar in the sky;
But they said, "Let's drop together
Down into that field so dry."

<hr>

So they jumped down, laughing and splashing
With a music fine and sweet,
And saved with their gracious moisture

The field of withering wheat.
Oh! my boys, come near while I tell you—
Let me speak as clear as I can:
'Tis little deeds, for wrong or right,
That will make or mar the man.

⊷═◉═⊶

Let your thoughts, your words, and your actions
Be honest and kind and true,
And the crown of a noble manhood
Will surely belong to you.

Talks to Boys

When You Grow Up

IF A BOY KNOWS WHAT TRADE, BUSINESS, OR PROFESSION HE wishes to have when he is a man, it is a very good thing. There is no doubt that he should follow his bent, and his education should be such as will help him best to develop those faculties which he will use in his work. But many a boy of good abilities, honest and sincere, does not know what he wants to be. It is for such boys that this article is written.

I feel sure that there is some particular work given to every one who is born into this world. And I think that if a boy will patiently and seriously study his own nature, in time he can find out what his work is. It is a good plan, in the first place, to find out what one can-not do. Many of the arts, for instance, require a genius— and that means more than a taste, or even a talent—for their successful pursuit. And there are at least two pro-fessions which should not be attempted unless one is sure of an unmistakable call toward them. A boy should never dare attempt to be a physician unless he has not only the strongest taste for the twin sciences of surgery and medicine, but also a love for humanity so broad and deep and unselfish that he cannot be satisfied with anything less than spending his lifetime in alleviating its miseries. And before he enters the Christian ministry he should be equally sure that he can be satisfied with no other life-work, and that he is willing to make the same self-consecration for the souls that a doctor does for the bodies of men.

Regarding what are called "the professions": never choose one because of the honor or distinction which it may bring you. No profession ever distinguished a man; on the contrary, if a man does not ennoble and dignify his profession he disgraces it.

Many pursuits are in these days barred out because they are not considered suitable for a gentleman. This is a mistake. All labor is honorable, and any man is a gentleman who behaves like one; and I know men today who have failed in life because they were put into a profession or a business, when if they had been allowed to learn their favorite trade or handicraft, they would have been successful and happy. So if you have a strong taste for anything of that sort, be sure it is a bent of your nature and not a fancy, then make your choice, stick to it, and be happy.

I know a gentleman, now living in a New England college town, where plain living and high thinking are yet the fashion, and he made such a choice and became a blacksmith; and he is the most wonderful blacksmith

I ever heard of. He has a power of subduing vicious animals which is phenomenal, and which two hundred years ago would have given him a reputation for sorcery. He shoes the most untamable horses entirely unaided; the touch of his hand, the sound of his voice, and the steady gaze of his bright dark eyes, in a short time after they are brought to him, quiet and subdue them and render them obedient to his will. This gentleman is a well-educated man, a reader and a thinker, and he is considered the social equal of anyone in the place; and I did not know whether to admire him more as he stood before his anvil, with his leather apron buckled on and his sleeves rolled up to his shoulders, displaying the magnificent muscles of his arm, while with his great hammer he smote with mighty blows the iron he was fashioning, making showers of sparks fly all about the place; or when, on the evening of the same day, he came forward to speak to me at the president's levee with the same easy and gentle manners with which he had welcomed me to his shop. And I imagine that if that man had attempted to be anything else than a blacksmith he would have disobeyed a divine call.

And when you have made your choice, remember that fitness for your business is not the only thing. Long years of steady work may be necessary before you gain success. Without industry, genius itself is nothing; but patient continuance in well-doing will surely win its reward.

≩ FOR FURTHER THOUGHT ≨

1. What is your favorite area of study in school—something you'd say you're good at?
2. Do you prefer to do things by yourself, such as read or use a computer, or would you rather do something with a group?
3. Which of these is easier for you to do?
   a. Follow instructions and put together something with your hands.
   b. Design something from your imagination, whether it's something to use or something just to look at.
   c. Express your ideas and thoughts by writing about them.
   d. Solve a problem or help someone else solve a problem.
4. If you could do any kind of work you wanted to do when you grow up, what would you choose to do?

A Talk to Business Boys

THE FIRST YEAR OF A BOY'S BUSINESS LIFE IS A CRITICAL ONE. He comes, perhaps, from a country home, certainly from a school-life well hedged about and protected by careful parents and teachers. He has lived heretofore [before this time] under conditions in which it was eas-

ier to go right than wrong, and it is indeed a change
when he takes life into his own hands and plunges into
a great city's business current, whose ramifications
encircle the world, and becomes one little atom in its
vast force. Then it is he gets his first practical experience of life and gains his first real knowledge of men
and things. Then, too, he begins to find out what metal
he himself is made of, and to shape his life's course;
and as he gives it an upward or a downward curve, so
it is apt to continue.

A boy's first position in a commercial house is usually at the foot of the ladder; his duties are plain, his
place is insignificant, and his salary is small. He is
expected to familiarize himself with the business, and
as he becomes more intelligent in regard to it he is
advanced to a more responsible place. His first duty,
then, is to his work. He must cultivate day by day habits
of fidelity, accuracy, neatness, and despatch [prompt-
ness], and these qualities will tell in his favor as surely
as the world revolves. Though he may work unnoticed
and uncommended for months, such conduct always
meets its reward.

I once knew a boy who was a clerk in a large mer-
cantile house which employed, as entry clerks, shipping
clerks, buyers, bookkeepers, and salesmen, eighty young
men, besides a small army of porters, packers, and truck-
men; and this boy of seventeen felt that amid such a
crowd he was lost to notice, and that any efforts he might
make would be quite unregarded. Nevertheless he did

his duty; every morning at eight o'clock he was promptly in his place, and every power that he possessed was brought to bear upon his work. After he had been with the firm a year he had occasion to ask them for the favor of a week's leave of absence during the busy season.

"That," was the response, "is an unusual request, and one which it is somewhat inconvenient for us to grant; but to show you that we appreciate the efforts you have made since you have been with us, we take pleasure in giving you the leave of absence for which you ask."

"I didn't think," said the boy, when he came home that night and related his success, "that they knew a thing about me, but it seems they have watched me ever since I have been with them."

They had indeed watched him, and had selected him for advancement; for shortly after he was promoted to a position of trust with an appropriate increase of salary.

It must be so, sooner or later, for there is always a demand for excellent work. A boy who means to build up for himself a successful business will find it a long and difficult task, even if he brings to bear his best efforts both of body and of mind; but he who thinks to win without doing his very best will find himself a loser in the race.

There is no position in life more honorable than that of a successful businessman, and there are few more influential. It is the judgment and advice of businessmen that guide affairs of national importance. The most wonderful inventions of the age are but serv-ants to do their bidding. It is no wonder that they are called "Railroad Kings" and "Merchant Princes," when we see the power they possess. How necessary, then, that the boys who are growing up to take the places of those men who now direct our commerce and manufactures, should be noble-hearted, honor-able, and intelligent men, not amassing wealth for its own sake or for the selfish pleasures which it brings, but to bestow it in a wise philanthropy for the com-fort, welfare, and advancement of their fellowmen.

⊰ FOR FURTHER THOUGHT ⊱

1. What do you think about the idea of giving your best effort to your work, without slacking off, even if no one sees you do it?
2. How do you feel inside when you do a good job?
3. Think of something you have to do at home every day or on a regular basis—make your bed, feed the dog, empty the trash. How could you do the job to your best ability? (*Hint:* Do it as neatly as possible; do it without being reminded. . . .)
4. How would doing a good job now help you when you grow up?

A Talk to Poor Boys

IF A BOY HAS GOOD HEALTH AND AN INTELLIGENT MIND, THE best thing that can happen to him is to have to make his own way in life; for every struggle increases his strength and every success gives him fresh courage and confidence, and whatever he wishes to be he can be. In this land of cheap books and free schools, if he desires an education he can get it. If he has a real thirst for knowledge, he can work his way through college as many another boy has done before him and enter any profession he chooses. So many of our distinguished men have fought this fight and have reached their present eminence entirely through their own exertions that it seems sometimes as if that was the only path to fame and honor, and as if all one had to do was to start at the bottom to end at the top; but the fact is that all poor boys do not become successful men. As Mr. Howells puts it, "I have known too many men who had *all* the disadvantage and who never came to anything." Those are the men who have neither the industry nor the pluck to work and fight through long years, if need be, until the battle is won.

The world is full of discontented and unhappy men, the cowards and deserters in the fight of life, lagging in the rear, hiding behind every shelter they can find, and grumbling because they cannot get somebody to fight and work for them. Envious of their neighbors who are better off, forgetting that other men have won their ease and comfort through their own industry and thrift, they blame everybody for their misfortunes except themselves. I do not know of what use such men are in this world, unless it be as warnings to the rising generation.

Never say you cannot do a thing because you have not the chance. If you really wish to do it and need to do it, the opportunity will come; and if you are swift to see it and quick to take it, it is yours.

But perhaps a boy who is reading this may say, "Ah, but I have more than myself to take care of. If I had only myself I could manage; but I have mother and the children, and I am the only man there is in the family." That is the best of all. A boy with such a trust never can nor will desert it; and he is learning daily such lessons of endurance, industry, and unselfishness as will be of priceless value to him during his whole life. Courage, my dear brave fellow, for you are sure to win.

A poor boy learns to "endure hardness like a good soldier," and things which others could not bear he takes as easily as a trained athlete lifts a weight which untrained muscles could not stir. So be thankful if you have been sent to school to Mistress Poverty, for though she is the sternest, yet she is the wisest and most faithful teacher, and if you will learn the tasks she sets, you will surely become a brave and noble man.

1. If you were a millionaire, how would you spend your money? Read Philippians 4:11-13. Do these Bible verses give you any new ideas about how you would spend your money?
2. In the story, the author says, "Never say you cannot do a thing because you have not the chance." What goal would you like to accomplish but feel it's beyond your reach? (*Hint:* Move up to the next reading group; get picked for the softball team; buy a computer.)
3. What could you do today to move toward that goal?

A Talk to Rich Boys

THERE IS NO DOUBT THAT TO BE THE SON OF A RICH FATHER is apt to be a disadvantage to a boy. He has all the clothes he needs, made of excellent material, well cut and suitable, his food is of the best, and the house in which he lives has every comfort and luxury. He has no anxiety about his school bills and he has plenty of money in his pockets. He is sent to the best of schools in the winter and goes to pleasant resorts in the summer or takes delightful journeys. His father and mother grant him every indulgence, and when he has finished college, where he has doubtless been lodged like a young Sybarite [a person devoted to luxury and pleasure], he is given every help that money can furnish to establish him in his chosen business or profession. All this is extremely hard on a boy. It is hard on him mentally, morally, and physically, and if he lives through it and comes out a noble man, he is indeed made of excellent metal. He knows nothing of anxiety or care, and he knows nothing of physical labor. He has no need of self-denial, industry, or endurance, and how can qualities which never are exercised be developed? I have read of a wealthy man who felt these things so keenly that after having given his son a liberal education, he shoved him out of the parental nest and made him shift for himself, and when he died left his fortune entirely to charity. I think he would have done better if he had educated that son as to the care, use, and value of money, and then left him the money as a sacred trust to be used both for himself and for his fellowmen. I feel sure that money was meant to be a blessing and not a curse, and that if we estimate it at its right value and use it as we should, it will prove to be so.

A rich boy, then, ought to be just as fine a fellow as a poor boy. Every virtue which a poor boy is obliged to cultivate if he makes a man of himself, a rich boy ought to cultivate for the same reason. He ought to rise superior to luxuries and to prove that if need be he can do without them. He should resist every temptation to dissipate and learn to work just as thoroughly and heartily as a poor boy must. Try during next vacation, if you are a rich boy, and see if you have sufficient pluck and knowledge to earn your own living. Insist always upon doing everything that you can for yourself. Play hard, work hard, and study hard, so as to fit yourself for the trust which is coming to you in your manhood. Remember that it is not the one who has the best start who wins the race, but the one who has the best staying power. You may have every possible advantage and help, but if you do not improve them they are of no benefit; for after all, you are the one who must make a man of yourself, and if you do not do it no one else can.

The annals of our country bear many honored names of men who never knew the sharp discipline of poverty, and who, being born with every advantage which wealth and position can give, realized that to these blessings were also added responsibilities—for from him to whom much is given much shall be required; and they nobly fulfilled their trust. They have left their mark upon the literature and art of their country. They have been in the van of noble reforms, and their philanthropy has been as wide as the land which they sought to benefit. And if a boy who has money will remember these things and will fit himself for that station in life to which it has pleased God to call him, his wealth will be a blessing to him and to the community in which he lives.

1. Describe how you feel when you buy something with money you've earned. How do you treat the thing you've purchased—baseball mitt, bicycle, computer software?

2. The author says that "it is not the one who has the best start who wins the race, but the one who has the best staying power." What is the author talking about when she uses the phrase "winning the race"?

3. How does the apostle Paul say we should view each day of our lives? (*Hint:* Read Philippians 3:12-14.)

A Talk to Schoolboys

I SUPPOSE MOST BOYS THINK THAT THE REASON WHY THEY ARE sent to school is to get an education, and that if they learn their lessons sufficiently well to pass the examinations and finish the prescribed course of study and be graduated, they will have that education and be ready for the business of life. But the object of the best schools nowadays is not simply the book-learning to be gained, but to give to a boy's spirit, mind, and body the best moral, mental, and physical training which he is capable of receiving, so that when school-days are ended a boy shall be equipped with a healthy and active body, a mind with alert perceptions and well-trained reasoning faculties, and a moral nature whose will is strong enough to govern both mind and body perfectly. This is a great deal to do, but it can be done if a boy will help his school to do it; and the way he can help is by his conduct. When a boy behaves well he always plays his fairest and studies his best, so that his mind and body and spirit are all being trained well together.

Every boy cannot carry off the first prize in his school for languages or mathematics, but every boy can be perfect in conduct if he will. And for the comfort of those boys who do not rank first in class I will say that although rank in class is always worth trying for, and every boy is bound to do his best, yet it is not always the most brilliant scholars who make the most successful men. I was reading not long since the experience of a gentleman who gained a part of his education at that historic institution, the oldest school in America, which is called the Boston Latin School. Says he: "I came home from this school at the end of the first month with a report which showed that I was ninth in a class of fifteen; that is about the average rank which I generally had. I showed it to my mother because I had to. To my great surprise and relief she said it was a very good report. I said I thought she would be displeased because I was so low in the class. 'Oh,' said she, 'that is no matter. Probably the other boys are brighter than you; God made them so and you cannot help that. But the report says you are among the boys who behave well. That you can see to, and that is all I care about.'"

That boy is now one of our wisest philanthropists and one of our most brilliant writers besides.

Every boy knows that he transacts a good deal of business during a school-term besides learning his lessons and playing his games. He has a great many plans and schemes which he is busy about. Perhaps he takes to taxidermy, and has various natural history collections of beast, bird, or fish. Or he plunges into mineralogy or botany with enthusiasm. Or he is occupied with private experiments in chemistry or inventions in mechanics, and all these things are excellent in their way and are as much a part of his education as his lessons. But it is on these points that I would like to give a gentle word of warning. For one thing, do not spend too much time on these things. Keep them in their proper place and they will rarely get you into trouble. Occasionally, however, something may go wrong through your inexperience or carelessness. It is surprising what a propensity things have to explode or to burn up, or at the least to make a very bad smell or to leave a dreadful stain, when they are being managed by a boy. Well, when you are in your scrape, own up and take the consequences and never attempt to slide out of it. You will have gained a valuable piece of experience, for I am sure you will never attempt to do that particular thing again in exactly that way, besides adding a bit of strength to your moral character by a temptation successfully resisted.

School-days are a delightful period of life. I don't say that they are the happiest times you will ever see, for I don't think that will be true; but it is true that your happiness and excellence as men depend greatly upon the use you make of your time while you are boys, for now you are building, habit by habit and thought by thought, the characters which you will have when you are men. So you should cherish now every generous aim and noble ambition which you would like to achieve as men, and scorn every mean and ignoble act now as cordially as you expect to do then, and practice every Christian virtue now as heartily as you mean to do then; and if you do these things you will be certain of a life which will bring happiness to yourself and a blessing to every one with whom it comes in contact.

⊰FOR FURTHER THOUGHT⊱

1. Why was the mother in the story not disappointed with the grades her son received?
2. Why do you think she was more pleased with good behavior than with straight A's?
3. Describe a person who has good character qualities. (*Hint:* What he thinks, says, and does every day.)

On Telling the Truth

THEY TEACH TWO THINGS AT WEST POINT WHICH I WISH WERE taught with equal thoroughness in every school in the land. One is to love the flag of our country, and the other is to speak the truth. The word of a cadet is accepted always unquestionably, but if he is detected in a falsehood he is dismissed from the service; and it would be well for every school if all were governed upon this point in a manner at once as trusting and as rigid.

Sometimes there comes a crisis in a boy's school or college life when a falsehood seems so easy and the truth so hard to tell—nobody knows how hard save the boy who has to tell it—that the sympathies of his friends would be very deep if they knew of the struggle; and if by writing this article I could help any boy who is in such a strait, I should be very glad.

Some time since I heard a boy who was in college giving his brother an account of a recent college scrape from which he had wisely retreated in time.

"You see," said the narrator, whom we will call Don for the time of this story, "we had settled on that night for 'the rush', and Prex got hold of it in some way; so he said in chapel that morning that no member of the Sophomore class should be out that evening after eight o'clock without being able to give a satisfactory account of himself. If he was out and was recognized, he would be expelled."

Now Don was at that time a Sophomore, and he was and is a lad with both a heart and a conscience, but he is so bubbling over with fun and brimming with life and vitality that his more valuable qualities are apt to be somewhat obscured.

"Well," he went on, "as soon as it got dark we rigged up so that it wouldn't be quite so easy for old Savage" (the college proctor) "to spot us, and we went out on the campus. All the fellows were there shrieking and howling and in for a good time and we were just getting formed into line when I felt someone touch me on the shoulder, and there was old Savage. 'Beg your pardon, Mr. B—,' says he as polite as you please, 'but I must request you to go at once to your room and to stay there. If you do not I shall be obliged to report your name to the president, and you know what the consequences will be.' And he warned all of the other fellows, too, but some he didn't call by name. You see Prex had told him to give us one more chance. Of course we all scattered, and some of us went in. I did, but oh, how I did hate to! But I knew it would be sure death if I did not, for Savage had my name listed, and I thought of mother; so I went up to my room and pegged away at my Greek all the evening. Some of the fellows came back later, and they were called before the Faculty and expelled, but there were a few that there wasn't any proof positive about, and some of them lied out of it, and they stayed. Well," continued

Don, sitting up and looking very earnest, "it was a falsehood they told, and no mistake. Every fellow in college knows it and Prex suspects it, but he can't prove it; and I look at them as they are going about, and I think they must feel mighty mean. But the question is, if I had been in their tight spot wouldn't I have done the same? I tell you, when expulsion comes so near as that, it looks like a very serious business. You think of the folks at home and all the trouble there will be there, and you don't have to tell on anybody else, you know. It is just to keep still about yourself, and it is very easy to do that and very hard to do the other thing. I'm glad I didn't have to choose; I'm glad I went in when old Savage told me to."

I thought then of another boy, whom I had known years ago, who had once to make that very choice, and who at the last moment chose the right and told the truth, though he then thought that it ruined his prospects for life. He had with a number of others transgressed the rules of his college, and he was summoned before the Faculty to answer the charges against him. A little deceit would have saved him, and one of the members of the Faculty, knowing it, suggested that he might not be reliable; but the boy turned to the old president, a man whom the greatest madcap among them loved and honored, and said, "I have never told you a lie yet, President F—, and I don't mean to begin now."

"That is quite sufficient," responded the president,

who knew the nature with which he was dealing, "I believe you. Proceed with your story."

The boy told it, was convicted, and expelled from the college. How he bore the shame and disgrace of that time he never could tell, but he was saved as by fire; and he left behind him with his college life his old foolish self and strove with all his might to make himself a noble man, and he succeeded. And I feel sure he would not have made the man he is today had he remained in college through his own deception and graduated at the expense of a lie. But he won his manhood through a bitter struggle, which he need not have fought if he had bravely resisted that sudden, sharp temptation which wrecked his college life.

I find that there are two morals to my talk this time. One is that it is never too late to mend. No matter how far you have gone astray, dare to turn around and do right at whatever cost, and you may be sure that it will be better for you both in this present life and in the life to come. And the second moral is—Do not do wrong in the first place. Never turn aside from the right track, for, after all, that is the nobler and wiser as well as the happier way.

⊰ FOR FURTHER THOUGHT ⊱

1. Why is it so tempting to lie when we've done something we shouldn't have?
2. Describe what the world would be like if no one ever lied.

3. Why is it important to tell the truth, no matter what
   the consequences (read Proverbs 12:14,19,22)?

On Spending and Saving

I ONCE KNEW TWO BROTHERS WHO WENT THROUGH COLLEGE
on exactly the same allowance. It was not an extrava-
gant allowance, neither was it scanty, but "'twas
enough, 'twould serve," if they were reasonably pru-
dent. It was paid to each lad quarterly, and they were
allowed to spend it just as they thought best. The elder
lad was always well dressed, had sufficient books, his
board-bill was promptly settled, and he always had a
surplus for amusements and incidentals. The other was
apt to look rather shabby, and he always had hard work
to make both ends meet. For about a week after he
received each allowance he lived in affluence; at the
end of that time he would thrust his two fists into his
empty pockets and inquire in blank despair, "Where
does the money go?"

"I've paid my paper bill and laundry bill," he
remarked on one occasion; "I've had a pair of shoes
mended; I've bought three neckties—I had to have
them—and 'pon my word I've only got one dollar and
sixty cents to last until next quarter-day."

Ben was a very bright and charming fellow and a

great favorite with his class, and when his check was cashed and the bills stowed away in his pocket, his first words were, "Come, fellows," and he would crack his first ten-dollar note in a treat. After that the bills would fly away right and left, some in perhaps a beautifully bound book or good engraving, or they would go in any amount of boyish trinkets, such as Russia leather card-cases, silver match boxes, elegant penknives, or the like. His father said nothing, for he had observed that in this case, talking did no good and he felt that experience must now be the teacher; and so it came to pass that Ben was stranded in the middle of a term, and left, as he expressed it, "gasping high and dry on the bank." He wrote to his father asking if he might draw a part of his next quarter's allowance in advance, but his father said, "No; what your brother Robert found to be sufficient you must make do."

He went to Rob, and Rob lent him ten dollars, which helped him for the moment; and then Ben went to his room and for the first time examined his accounts and faced the situation. He was in debt, and deeply in debt for the size of his income. His whole coming quarter's allowance would not cover his liabilities. He recalled more than one warning of his father's on the subject of indebtedness, and he began to realize that he had behaved in a very dishonorable manner, for he knew that his father gave him all the money he could afford. He sat staring at the opposite wall, where hung a fine little etching which was his last extravagance, and wondered what he should do. His father clearly would not help him, and could not in justice if he would. And Ben was quite at the end of his rope. But he had good stuff in him. When he had been made to stop and think, he thought to some purpose. All at once he started as if he had been stung, and springing up, he began to walk rapidly up and down the room with his brows knit. "I'll do it," he said, and crushing on his hat he ran downstairs and out of doors with an air of great resolution.

The fact was that the proprietor of the steam laundry which he patronized had asked him a few days before if he knew of any student who would like to keep his books for him. The hours of work were from seven to nine in the evening, and the compensation was fair; and Ben put his pride in his pocket, applied for this situation, and got it. Great was the astonishment of his mates at this singular move of his, but he persevered and earned the money, and with it he succeeded in paying his debts; and by the end of the year he could look his father in the eyes without any shame or trouble, for he stood fair and square with all the world.

But there are many other things in this world beside money which can be saved or spent. Many a lad needs to think of how he spends his time.

This same Ben—who I may as well admit is one of my "best boys," in spite of his faults—sometimes remarks that "Punctuality is the thief of time!" "Look at Rob," he says; "he is always *there*. He was never known to be late at a class or a lecture or a committee meeting in his life. But think of the things he misses because he is always in such a tearing hurry, while I acquire quantities of information simply by keeping my eyes open and taking things easy. Depend upon it, the fetlock [foot or ankle] is the place to take old Time by, instead of snatching the hair off his head as some folks do."

Nevertheless, Master Ben is finding out that if he ever makes a mark in the world he cannot indulge in a wasteful extravagance of time any more than he can of money, and I am glad to see that he is settling down to his working life quietly, patiently, and perseveringly.

These things will bear thinking about, and the boy who spends not only his money, but his time, prudently is really braver as well as better than those who do not.

⊰ FOR FURTHER THOUGHT ⊱

1. When you get paid for chores or for working a job, what's the first thing you think about doing with the money?
2. What's your favorite thing to do when there's nothing you absolutely have to do?
3. Think of ways you spend time that are like the way you spend money.

On Plain English

NOT VERY LONG SINCE, ONE OF MY BOY FRIENDS DROPPED IN, as he is apt to do during vacation, to spend an hour or so with me. I have known him ever since he was a little fellow, but since he has been away at school I have not seen so much of him. On the afternoon of which I speak he began to talk to me about his school life, and I should have been very glad to listen if I had been able to understand him; but two years of school, while it may have improved his Latin and Greek, seemed to have quite removed from him the power of using plain English. His father and mother are people of cultivation and refinement, and during his childhood he had been used to hearing the English language spoken with great purity; but his conversation on this occasion was so corrupted with slang that I was obliged to interrupt him frequently to ask him what certain expressions meant, and I noticed that he had some difficulty in telling me. The only synonyms which occurred to his mind were other slang words or phrases which were quite as unintelligible to me as the first. He seemed rather embarrassed by his difficulties and said he "never could talk, anyhow, unless he was with a lot of fellows. He didn't know how to talk to other people."

It seemed rather a pity for a bright young lad of sixteen to have to confess such a thing, and what made the case peculiar was that he was one of the best orators of his school, and he had just written and delivered a prize oration which was excellent; but the trouble was that he had allowed himself to talk in such a slipshod manner among his mates for so long that he was unable to express himself properly in ordinary conversation.

I was talking with a certain liberal professor of English literature once on this subject, and he remarked that "slang ought not to be frowned down altogether, for the language is constantly being enriched by new words and expressions which were once called slang, but are now by common consent considered correct English. The words and phrases which are worthless will be cast aside, and those which are valuable will in a few years be incorporated into the language and be in constant use."

I smiled and said, "Perhaps you are right."

But when a lad "enriches" his mother tongue to such an extent that middle-aged people cannot understand him, when he uses slang without knowing it and makes slang words and phrases the chief part of his vocabulary, he makes a mistake, for he defiles the wells of pure English from which he might draw to suit his needs, and which are a rich inheritance to him from the great storehouse of the past; and while I should be the last to repress those witty and forcible expressions which boys have a genius for coining, and which, as the professor remarked, are of genuine value, I cannot but think that there is a great deal of slang which is both vulgar and meaningless and which it is a great pity for any boy to make use of.

There is another point to which it is well to pay attention. Very few of us take the trouble to pronounce correctly even if we know how. Just watch yourself a little and see whether you say *wy* or *why*; and do you always say *and*, or do you sometimes say *an'*, and do you invariably sound *ing* distinctly, or do you defraud word endings by saying *in'*? Many people, if they should see the words they use written as they speak them, would be shocked indeed, and it is only because we are more used to hearing incorrect English spoken than we are to seeing it written, that we do not notice our mistakes. It is only after hearing it spoken by a master that we realize what a noble and beautiful tongue our English is. It is generally conceded that there is no language which is at once so copious, so flexible, and so suited for the expression of ideas; and yet there are many people whose mother tongue it is, and who speak it all their days, who never realize its worth and who go through life poverty-stricken for want of words with which to express their thoughts, their feelings, and their desires.

⊰ FOR FURTHER THOUGHT ⊱

1. Slang words will always be with us, and sometimes they get put in the dictionary as part of the official English language. Why, then, does it matter how "properly" you speak?

2. Some words are more fun to say than other words,
   like *sassafras* and *hippopotamus*. Take a look
   through the dictionary and choose a word to use in
   conversation this week. Make it a game with your
   family and see who becomes the best at finding fun
   words to say.

On Weak Points

LAST HOLIDAY, WHEN THE ACADEMY TERM WAS ENDED, I
asked Harry how he ranked. "Well," said he, "my average is only fair, for though I am well up in my languages, yet I do so hate mathematics that I am always
at the very bottom of the class with them, so, of course,
that pulls down my general average; but in Latin"—and
he smiled—"I am leading the crowd."

"Then you really enjoy the languages?" said I,
"and they come easy to you?"

"Oh, yes," he answered readily. "I like them ever
so much."

"Which do you give the most time to," I asked,
"your Latin or your Algebra?"

"Why, my Latin, of course," he answered, surprised. "I won't bother about my Algebra any more
than I must."

"Ah, but you are making a mistake," said I. "It is

precisely because you don't like it and don't take to it naturally that you ought to cultivate it. You should spend three times as much time on your Algebra as you do on your Latin. You have as much sense as the average boy, and if you would apply yourself you could comprehend mathematics as well as any one; your brain needs just that clear and exact habit of thought which can be cultivated by a mathematical training and nothing else, and you will miss it all your life if you do not take it now while you can get it."

But Harry hopelessly shook his head. "I can never do anything at it; it is no use to try."

"Harry," said I, "you began to tell me a little while since of that friend of yours with the weak chest, and how slender and round-shouldered he was when he began at the Academy, and you said he had no muscle whatever; and you told me how he took to practicing every day in the gymnasium with the rowing-machine and with boxing-gloves. Seems to me that was very silly for a fellow like him."

"Why, no," answered Harry, alert in a minute, for he admires "muscle" above all things. "Why, no. You just ought to see him now. His chest has expanded five inches, and his biceps—they are as hard as rocks, and he is as straight in the back as anybody. It was just the thing for him."

"Exactly," I answered, smiling, "and I wish that you would show as much sense in the training of your mind as your friend has in the training of his body.

You would find the results quite as admirable if you would treat your brain to a course of mathematical athletics. You would find that portion of your brain cells which you would be forced to use improved, strengthened, and quickened by use quite as much as the flaccid muscles of your friend's body were improved by his exercise."

My boys who read this, I don't know what your weak points may be, but I know that you have them, for there never was a character in this world—save One—that was perfectly symmetrical and strong at every point. But this I do know, that it is possible for you to make your weak point, whatever it may be, the very strongest point of your character, for there you know that you are liable to be tempted; so there you can be perpetually on guard, so that it will be impossible for the enemy to surprise you, and there—God helping you—you can always win the fight.

⊰FOR FURTHER THOUGHT⊱

1. The author says we should spend more time doing the thing that is hardest for us to master. What do you think you need to spend more time on?
2. According to the author, how is it possible "to make a weakness the very strongest point of your character"?
3. Who or what is your greatest source of help when you are weak (2 Corinthians 12:9-10)?

The Soul of Honor

THERE IS A CERTAIN QUALITY OF THE MORAL NATURE WHICH IS called honor. The dictionary defines it as "true noble-ness of mind, springing from probity, principle, or moral rectitude," and calls it "a distinguishing charac-teristic of good men." Such a quality will bear thinking about a little.

The other day a certain wealthy gentleman, speak-ing of a young man in his employ, said, "I would trust him with every dollar I possess. He is the soul of honor."

These were not idle words, for I knew he was in the habit of confiding to that young man large busi-ness interests which involved a great deal of capital; I knew, too, that he had no security for his money; he "trusted him."

Once in a large boys' school a disturbance occurred which involved nearly a whole class. The master sent for the principal of the school. He entered the room and listened to the teacher's account of the trouble; then, glancing around at the pupils, he said, "I should like to know exactly how this happened, so I will ask Fred B— to tell me."

Fred stood up and related the occurrence from beginning to end clearly and fairly, naming no names, but taking his share of the blame, and then sat down.

"Now," said the principal, "I should like the other boys who have been implicated in this trouble to follow Fred's example and acknowledge it as he has done." And the other lads arose and owned up also.

Afterwards in speaking of the affair the principal said, "I knew I could rely upon Fred to tell me the exact truth without fear or favor, for though he may be led astray in a moment of excitement, he is always willing to acknowledge when he has done wrong. There is nothing underhanded or mean about him. I have tried him and tested him often, and he is regarded by both his classmates and teachers as the soul of honor."

It is somewhat rare, and it certainly is a very beautiful thing, to have a reputation such as this young man possessed, and it is something worth striving one's whole life long to win; and yet such a character is built of very little things. Many people who would indignantly deny that they ever told a falsehood, nevertheless seem quite incapable of relating a thing exactly as it occurred. They will either enlarge or detract or vary the statement in some way, so that their words are not reliable. And many a lad in business who would not take a dollar from his firm unlawfully, will yet take that firm's stamps and letter-paper for his private correspondence. The firm will never feel it, it is true, but that lad's character will feel it; and the boy who habitually does such things will in the end find his conscience so blunted that dishonesty will come easy to him, and he will not be able to withstand some sudden, sharp temptation, and he will fall. Those who do not know him well will be surprised; but those who know his real life will know that for years his character has been undermined by trifling deceptions and dishonesties, just as the ocean slowly encroaches upon a sandy shore, and at last, during some terrible storm, when the wind is raging, it will gather itself in its might and wash inland, bearing devastation and death and changing the whole face of the country.

The lad who cheats a little in his games or remains silent while others cheat; he who learns his lessons with a "crib," or takes his diagrams or dates into class upon his cuffs, or gets his answers from his neighbor— yes, and the boy who gives such unlawful help too— they are dishonorable boys, and it would be better for them if they had never been born than to live on and grow up and carry into life such principles as these. But no boy means to do that. He means to do it "just once," because he is hard pressed for some reason. Think a minute. Did you never do it but once? The boy who does it once is very apt to do it again, and to go on doing such things until they become the habit and practice of his life. Therefore a boy should be very watchful that no petty deceit or dishonesty ever stains his life, and to behave in all things so truly and so nobly that those who know him best and love him dearest can proudly and gladly say of him, "He is the soul of honor."

⊰ FOR FURTHER THOUGHT ⊱

1. What's wrong with taking an extra pencil home from the school supply cupboard or looking at someone's test paper for just one answer?
2. What happens to you inside when you do something dishonest "just once"?
3. What's the danger of letting small instances of dishonesty creep into your life?

Reading for Life

THE BEST BOOK OF ALL TO READ IS OF COURSE THE BIBLE. IT is the most interesting book in the world. Almost anyone would admit that, and yet I know that if I should put the question "honor bright" to some of the boys who read this article, they would answer honestly that they do not think so. This is partly because they have not learned to read the Bible properly.

Many people read the Bible in a piecemeal sort of way, a chapter every night before they go to bed, and they bring up their children to do the same. Now a few verses from the Bible are a very good thing to go to sleep on, but one will never get a real knowledge of the book by reading it in that way only. Such reading is for rest and comfort, but it is not for information. And how many of you who read in that fashion remember from one night to another what you read? The end of a chapter does not by any means necessarily conclude the subject of which it treats, or even indicate a good place for stopping, for the narrative or argument may be continued through several chapters, or indeed to the end of the book. You should give the Bible as fair a chance to interest you as you give any other book, and any other book you read connectedly from beginning to end. Suppose next Sunday afternoon when you are neither tired nor sleepy, but when you feel just in the mood for a good comfortable read, instead of taking up your Sunday school book or a religious paper, you settle yourself with your Bible and read the Acts of the Apostles from the first verse to the last, and when you have finished it you will have a realizing sense of the courage and devotion of the men whom Christ chose to plant His church; and Peter and Paul and James and John will seem like live men to you, and real heroes too, and you will want to trace their lives from beginning to end.

By reading a book through you get a clear idea of the author's design, and you are able to appreciate the beauty and force of the language which he uses.

Another good way to read the Bible is to take it by subjects. The Old Testament biographies are exceedingly interesting. Take the life of Moses or Joseph or David and read it through, and you will be sure to like it. After you have once begun to enjoy the Bible I am sure you will never leave off. You will read it more and love it better and better the longer you live, and the better you become acquainted with it the more you will wonder at its inexhaustible riches.

After the Bible the next best thing for a boy to read is a good newspaper. Newspapers are the publishers of modern history. They bring the history of our own times to us every morning, and every great question which affects the welfare of mankind is reflected in them. It is not necessary to read about the commitment of horrible crimes or the execution of criminals, or topics of that nature, but you do want to know about the history of the last strike, for instance, because it concerns the great struggle between capital and labor which you are to help decide in a few years. You should keep track of the doings of Congress and the gist of the President's messages and international legislation, and foreign topics you should not miss. Think of the things which have happened abroad this past year, the centennial jubilees, the death of kings and eminent statesmen. One cannot pass these things by. Besides all this, the latest discoveries in every science are reported in the newspapers, the explorations of unknown countries are mirrored there, descriptions of the best and newest works in literature, in music, are in its columns, and to read the newspapers is in itself a liberal education. Therefore I would advise every boy who is too busy to give much attention to general literature, to read carefully the news of the day, for if he does he cannot fail of being an intelligent man, and then, when a time of leisure comes, he will have an excellent foundation to build upon when he is able to cultivate his mind more thoroughly.

⊰For Further Thought⊱

1. What is the most important book you can read?
2. How does the author recommend you should read the Bible?
3. Why does the author place so much importance on newspapers (or reading news on the Internet if you're a computer buff)?

On Reading Books

What books should our boys read? That is a wide question. There are quantities of charming books nowadays which are published on purpose for young people, many of which are both delightful and instructive. Dear old *Tom Brown at Rugby,* for instance, is one of the best of friends and companions for any boy. But I should not advise a boy to depend upon this class of literature. I believe in reading for profit as well as for pleasure, and the best results will be obtained by cultivating an acquaintance with general English literature.

There are three sorts of boys in this world: those

with a healthy appetite for good wholesome reading, which they take to as naturally as they do to beefsteak and potatoes; those who because of various circumstances have not been thrown much with books and who think that they do not like to read, though they really do not know whether they do or not; and lastly those whose taste has become debased by reading the trashy, exciting, cheap literature which has inundated the country like a flood, until other books seem stale and flat to them. Now this article is chiefly for the two latter sorts of boys, and for the last mentioned class I am particularly sorry, because they are not very well in their minds, and I would like to cure them if I could. I wish I could make every boy who reads this understand the unspeakable delight which comes from reading a good book; then I should be sure that whatever else might fail him in the way of earthly joys, he would be sure of one great happiness and consolation.

Boys who are in business particularly need to cultivate the habit of reading because they are apt to leave school early, and if they are not careful they will become so absorbed in the fierce competition which now characterizes all sorts of business that by the time they are twenty-five they will care for nothing else, and by the time they are fifty they will be in the condition of a poor man whom I once knew, who, broken in health, but with more money than he could use, still dragged himself daily to business and went on making more, because, as he pitifully remarked, he did not know what else to do.

"But," says my business boy, who works nights during the busy season and who doesn't like reading, "do you suppose that I could study English literature?"

Certainly I do. A boy who can spare on an average an hour a day for reading will be able to read a good deal in the course of the year.

"But," says my boy who doesn't like reading, "I can't bear poetry."

When a boy says that to me I always try him with "Horatius at the Bridge," or Tennyson's ballad of "The Revenge." If he does not like either of those poems I conclude that he is right in his own estimate of his taste; but I never met a boy who did not like such poetry.

"Well," says my boy again, "history is awfully dull. I never can remember the dates."

But, I answer, you can remember the century in which the events occurred, and that will do very well. Try it with Green's *Shorter History of the English People,* and see if you cannot. For essays, try Charles Dudley Warner's "Being a Boy," and you will discover that an essay is not necessarily a dull and uninteresting thing, "as dry as a chip," as many a boy supposes. For biographies take, perhaps, James T. Fields' *Yesterdays With Authors,* or Noah Brooks' *Historic Boys,* or *Sea Kings and Naval Heroes,* by J. G. Edgar. For a story of travel and adventure take Lieutenant Greely's *Three Years of Arctic Service.* You will not understand all of the scientific allusions, but if your heart does not beat fast by the time you have finished reading how Lieutenant Lockwood with his two devoted companions won the "Farthest North," then you are not the boy I take you for. For novels there is gallant Sir Walter Scott, one of my childhood's very best friends. If you do not know him, you had best read *Ivanhoe* right away.

The best short story that I know of for boys is Edward Everett Hale's "Man Without a Country."

And now, my boy who "doesn't like to read," if you should read one of the articles or books in each class which I have named, do you realize that you would have had a taste of history, biography, essays, poetry, and novels? and these are the component parts of general English literature. And after having taken a taste you will discover that the table is spread and you have only to help yourself wisely and judiciously to whatever you please; and the habit of reading good books when once formed, besides giving a great deal of pleasure, cannot fail to make you a cultivated man, whether you have had the advantage of being trained in the schools or not.

⊰ FOR FURTHER THOUGHT ⊱

1. What is your favorite book or story? Why?
2. Why are you fortunate all your life if you are a reader of books?

Recommended Guides for Selecting Children's Books

Books Children Love: A Guide to the Best Children's Literature by Elizabeth Wilson, Crossway Books, 1987.

Eyeopeners! How to Choose and Use Children's Books about Real People, Places, and Things by Beverly Kobrim, Penguin Books, 1988.

On Self-Control

THERE IS NO QUALITY A BOY ADMIRES MORE THAN THAT OF self-control, and it is right to admire it, for it is only the man who has control of himself who can control others and can be of value and service to the community in which he lives.

No one can hear untouched such a story, for instance, as that of the English troopship which sprung a leak, and the officers and men, when they found they could not save her, safely and quickly transferred their wives and children to the boats, and then, drawn up at quarters, each man at his post, quietly and calmly went down with the ship, content with having saved the lives which were dearer to them than their own.

The heroic endurance of pain, the ready wit in an emergency, the lightning-like quickness of thought which plans, and the steady hand which executes a rescue, such traits command the respect and admiration of everyone, and every boy wishes that he could possess them. Boys, and older people too, are apt to think that these qualities are an especial gift, like a genius for music or art, and that no one can behave in this way unless it is, as the phrase goes, "born in him." It is true that to some self-control comes easier than to others, but it is without doubt a quality which can be cultivated. You can have it or not as you choose.

A friend of mine who was a volunteer during the late war, though at that time he was scarcely more than a lad, was relating to a few friends something of his experience. He is one of the most quiet, retiring, and gentle of men, not at all a man whom one would suspect of having soldier stuff in him.

"Were you never afraid?" someone asked him curiously.

"Yes," he answered frankly, "I was always afraid. I never went into a fight in my life that I did not tremble just in the beginning, and any minute I would have been glad to run for old Vermont. But," with a little smile, "I didn't do it. I suppose," he continued, turning to me, "that you would call me a coward."

"If you had run away," I answered, "perhaps I should; but my idea of a brave man is not one who does not know the meaning of the word *fear,* but rather one who knows the feeling, and who conquers it, and does his duty just the same."

I could not say to his face what I knew to be a fact, that he had won promotion three times for conspicuous gallantry upon the field of battle, and that he had inspired his men with such confidence in him that they would follow anywhere he led.

Therefore if a boy feels that he is lacking in self-control, the best thing he can do is to practice it every chance he gets. There are several young men of my acquaintance who faint at the sight of blood, and when there is an accident in their vicinity they, every one of them, get out of the way, because if they are called upon to help they may drop at just the most critical minute. They all regard the trait as constitutional, but it is my belief that if they would exert their will power sufficiently they could conquer their infirmity.

There is nothing more desirable than the ability to keep cool in case of an accident, and it is well to have some idea of what to do until the doctor comes. There are several excellent little books which are printed for this purpose. After he comes, do exactly what he tells you. He will never ask you to do anything which you cannot do if you pay strict attention, control yourself, and try.

The best way to maintain self-control in an emergency is to always keep control of yourself when there is no emergency; that is, to practice it all the time, for one has plenty of opportunity in everyday life. Keep your temper through every game, no matter how exciting. When someone else wins the prize which you have been striving for during the whole term, shake hands with the victor and say, "I'm glad you have won it." If a sudden insult comes, which seems to make every

drop of blood in your body boil indignantly to the sur-
face, clinch your teeth until you can answer calmly, or
do not speak at all. Never allow yourself to become so
excited that you do not know what you are about. Train
the hands and feet and eyes and brain to constantly
serve you well, and then they will not fail you in time
of trouble; and you will find that in sudden need,
instead of being paralyzed with fright and helpless, you
can think and act with a quickness and capacity which,
when it is all over, will seem surprising even to yourself; or if it should be your lot to bear instead of to do,
you can endure with a composure which will be a comfort to yourself and to all of your friends.

⊰ FOR FURTHER THOUGHT ⊱

1. How do you react when you lose a game? When
   someone says something mean to you? When you
   get scared?
2. What does it mean to have a "cool head"?
3. How can you practice having a cool head in any
   situation?

Which Was the Braver?

THEY WERE LOOKING AT THE ICE ON THE RIVER ONE DAY
early in the winter. The ponds were frozen and the

Branch was frozen, but no one yet had had a skate on
the deep and rapid river, and all the boys were aching
to try it. It lay before them frozen from shore to shore,
a smooth expanse of dark and glassy ice, most tempting to the sight of any boy, and to the little group of
lads who stood eyeing it, it was almost irresistible. They
had been skating on the Branch, so they had their
skates in their hands, and every now and then one of
them would venture out upon the ice and stamp about
to try it. At last one lad came back from one of these
short excursions.

"Pooh!" said he, stamping, "it's safe, safe enough
for an elephant, and I am going to try it. I dare any one
of you fellows to skate across with me. Dare, dare,
double dare you, Fritz Ward, to do it," and down he sat
to put on his skates. "What!" said Jack, "nobody coming? Not you, Fritz Ward? The champion skater of the
town refuses. Well, well!"

"No, I'm not going," answered Fritz.

But his refusal was not because he was afraid or
because he did not want to go, for he was all eagerness
to be off; but he had promised his mother that he
would not go on the river until it had been pronounced
perfectly safe, and he never yet had broken his word to
her, and that was all that held him.

Jack was cutting airy circles near the shore and
watching them, smiling.

"Well, good-by, 'fraid cats," said he, and giving his
hand a little mocking flourish, off he flew straight

toward the middle of the river, and his light, boyish figure seemed to skim the ice like a bird; but light as he
was, it bent beneath him as he sped. The lads on the
bank saw it and cried, "Come back," but he never
heeded, in fact he was afraid to turn, and in another
instant down he went. His comrades stared as if they
were dreaming at that little black hole in the ice where
Jack went down; and though those boys now are
middle-aged men, yet they can shut their eyes, any one
of them today, and see again that snow-clad shining
landscape, and the gleaming river with that little black
hole in it well out toward the middle. It was but an
instant when they saw Jack's head once more, and his
face was turned toward them. He threw his arms out
on to the ice and it broke beneath his weight, but
before he sank he grasped it again with his other arm
and it bore him for a moment, only to break again, but
it brought him a little nearer to his friends. Instantly
he comprehended what he had to do. He had to break
his way bit by bit through the ice across that dreadful
river. His friends could not help him, so like the gallant lad he was, he fought on inch by inch for his life,
while his friends on shore cheered him all they could.

"Fellows," said Fritz Ward, watching him keenly,
"he will never reach us without help; take off your
comforters"—they all wore worsted scarves knotted
around their necks, and each of them was fully two
yards long. "Knot them together tightly," Fritz continued. "I know the bottom here, and I am going out

as far as I can to meet him. I shall throw him these and you must help me. I am going in up to my waist, and you must all throw yourselves on your faces and work yourselves out one after the other. Each fellow hang on to the other, and you, Joe Anderson, come next to me and steady me."

It was planned and done in a minute. Fritz, with the coil of comforters ten yards long, went out until the ice cracked beneath him, and then he let himself down into the water. Joe Anderson, who was the lightest boy there, had cautiously worked himself out and lay near enough to give a steadying hand to Fritz, who was in up to his armpits, but his arms were free.

"Just a little nearer, old boy," shouted Fritz to Jack, "and I'll throw it," and poor Jack struggled a moment more. "Now," cried Fritz, and threw the rope, and the end lay well within Jack's reach. He grasped it and Fritz drew him inch by inch through the splintering ice until he had him by the collar; then the ice broke under Joe and let him down, but he landed on his feet, and together he and Fritz tied one end of the comforters under Jack's arms and tossed the other end to the other boys. Then somehow they got him on to the ice, and the other boys pulled him cautiously ashore. After that Fritz and Joe were helped out, and the dry boys piled their overcoats on to the wet boys, and they took Jack, who was by that time quite unconscious, safe home.

When Jack was convalescing from his attack of

pneumonia the first boy he wanted to see was Fritz. He held out his hand to him with a smile.

"Old boy," said he, "if it hadn't been for you I wouldn't be here."

"Pshaw!" answered Fritz, "it was the comforters did the business."

"Ah!" said Jack, "the comforters were a very good thing, but I would never have got hold of them if it hadn't been for you. You need not try to get out of it. If you hadn't been as quick as thought and chock full of pluck beside, I wouldn't be in this world now. And the sense you've got too, Fritz," Jack went on reflectively; "first time I ever knew you not to take a dare. How did it happen?"

"Oh," answered Fritz, laughing, "that was not any sense of mine. I would have been after you fast enough if I hadn't promised my mother that I wouldn't go on the river that day."

"Well," said Jack, "my old doctor says there is a difference between courage and foolhardiness, and it is pretty plain which quality he thinks I have shown the most of recently; but in the future I am going to keep what little courage I have left to use when it is needed, instead of fooling it away in such a scrape as this."

All this happened years ago, but the lesson Jack then learned has never been forgotten. He has had plenty of battles to fight since then, and he has fought them bravely; but his old foolhardy, daring ways, which so threatened to injure his character, he left behind him forever on that terrible day when he fell through the ice into Green River.

⊰For Further Thought⊱

1. Has anyone ever dared you to do something dangerous? How did you handle the dare?
2. In the story, who do you think was more courageous, the boy who went out on the ice or the boy who refused to take a dare?
3. How does the author define "courage" in the story? Do you agree?

A Danger Signal

ONCE, WHEN I WAS A LITTLE GIRL, I TOOK A DRIVE THAT I SHALL never forget. A party of us were going to attend the commencement exercises of a college situated about three miles from the town in which we lived. Our own carriage was filled with guests and driven away, and my mother and I accepted seats in the carriage of a neighbor. This neighbor's horses were a pair of frisky young colts—beautiful, spirited creatures—not long since broken to the harness, and the gentleman who undertook to drive us was a friend from a distance who was little accustomed to the management of horses; but no trouble was apprehended, as the horses were not at all vicious and the roads were excellent. We had proceeded only a short distance, however, when we noticed that the horses did not go with their usual fine, steady gait. They began to prance and fret and to act decidedly nervous. Our driver only irritated them by his efforts to control them, and at last they broke away and dashed into a run. My mother clasped me close as we whirled along, the light buggy swaying and rocking dangerously over every inequality of the road, when suddenly, just as we were giving ourselves up for lost, a young fellow with the figure of an athlete sprang out from the roadside, seized the horses by their heads, and with one powerful movement turned them toward the fence and stopped them. They were quivering in every nerve, and with the touch and tone of a born horseman he began to soothe them, meanwhile examining the harness with a knowing eye.

"Why," said he, "these horses are hitched up wrong. It is no wonder they ran away." And he began altering straps and buckles to rectify the mistake.

By this time the horses were much quieted and my mother had recovered herself, and she called the young gentleman to her side. I shall never forget his bright, gallant face and his noble bearing as he came forward to receive the thanks with which she overwhelmed him. My mother then took me on her lap, and our preserver, seating himself beside us, drove us safely to the college.

This was the beginning of our acquaintance with this young man, and it will not harm him now if I give the history of that acquaintance until its close. It may perhaps serve as a sort of danger signal to some other young man who is possessed of a similar temperament and who is beginning to travel in the way he went. Let us call him for the time of this story Harry Belden.

After the college exercises were concluded my mother spoke to the president, who was an old and much valued friend of our family, and related our adventure, and spoke in warm terms of our preserver.

"Ah," responded he, "it was Harry Belden, was it? I wish, Mrs. H—, that you would invite him to your house."

"I have already done so," said my mother, somewhat surprised. "He is coming to tea tomorrow evening."

"He is the son of my old friend Horace Belden, of L—," explained the president, speaking somewhat gravely. "He is to spend his vacation with me at my house, and next fall he enters college. The fact is, he is somewhat dissipated, and I have promised my friend Belden to do what I can for him, so he is to be under my own eye, and we hope a good deal from a quiet country life. He's a charming fellow, charming," he added emphatically, "and he is too young to be lost. I shall be glad for him to have your house to go to, for it is a cheerful place, and he will enjoy it."

Every tender feeling in my mother's heart was roused for this young fellow who had saved her life and that of her child, and yet was so near to making shipwreck of his own. She and my father made him thoroughly welcome at our home, and as the president had prophesied, he did enjoy it. My two young lady aunts who resided with us filled the house with life and joy, and Harry Belden's frequent visits made the bright summer days seem brighter still. He was indeed a "charming fellow," bubbling over with wit and mirth, generous, kind-hearted, and obliging, and gifted with a handsome face and manners of a thorough gentleman. I do not think that in all his life he had known, or that he ever did know in after years, the sensation of physical fear. A thing to be really enjoyable to him must have a spice of danger; a situation that would justly alarm another but produced a sense of exhilaration in him. It was but a pleasurable excitement. It brought his "blood up," as he himself expressed it, and then whose foot so fleet, whose hand so firm, whose nerve so steady as his? Of course, possessing such a disposition, he excelled in all manly exercises. A good shot, a fine rider, an excellent swimmer, and devoted to athletic games, in all these things he was more than fine; he was recklessly daring. But, alas! this craving for excitement was his ruin; it made all simple, normal pleasures seem dull and tame, and he turned to intoxicating drink for satisfaction. He understood the danger he was in and appreciated President F—'s efforts in his behalf. June and July had gone by, and the last days of August were come, and still Harry Belden had made no slip from the right path, and his friends were hoping that a reform had really begun. But, alas! one August evening he did not return home as usual; nine, ten o'clock passed, and still he did not come. Then President F— drove down to the town and instituted a search through its liquor saloons, and in one of them Harry Belden was discovered almost dead drunk. He was assisted into the buggy and taken home and cared for by his kind friend. When he came to himself he was very penitent, and the grief and disappointment of the dear old "Prex," as the boys all called him, affected him greatly.

"I'm not worth it, sir," he said to him. "You would much better let me go."

But President F— would not let him go; he called upon him by every sense of duty and honor that he possessed to fight the demon which had conquered him, and he promised to try again. Perhaps the most discouraging thing about him was the ready way in which he would promise to cooperate with any efforts which were made for his reform; for with the first sharp temptation he would break every promise, and yield apparently without an effort.

Autumn came and the students returned to college, and Harry joined the Sophomore class. He proved to have a quick and retentive mind, and the president hoped that the necessity of steady and regular work would be of benefit to him; but far from it. As soon as the novelty of his position had faded he began to associate with the worst characters of the class, and one night under his leadership they indulged in a wine supper, which ended in such a scene of debauchery as was a disgrace to the whole college. This could not be overlooked; it was a case for expulsion, and Harry knew it.

"It's no use, sir," said he to the president. "I told you so months ago; but don't think that I do not remember your kindness to me. I do, though I have abused it so shamefully."

Harry Belden went home to his parents, and we never saw him again; but the rest of his sad story can be told in a few words. He made two or three futile efforts to reform after this, and during one of them he married a lovely young girl of his native city. She had but a few months of happiness; he fell again, and deserted her, going to a distant city. There, under an assumed name, he married another young lady. But his fraud was soon discovered, and he is now serving out a sentence for bigamy in the prison of his native State.

This is a sad story to read. It has been a sad story to write. And if it were not for the hope of arresting some careless footsteps which are beginning to tread the downward path that Harry Belden trod, it would never have been written.

People used to say in a kind of sad excuse for Harry's doings that "he was his own worst enemy." This was pitifully, shamefully true; for, with all his courage and his daring, there was one person whom he never dared to face, and in whose presence he was a miserable coward, and that person was himself. If he had sought the aid of our best and ever-present Friend, resolved to conquer his evil impulses and desires at whatever cost, he would have been today a noble man, honored, respected, and beloved by all who knew him, instead of what he is, a poor miserable felon.

⊰ FOR FURTHER THOUGHT ⊱

1. What did it mean in the story when people said Harry was "his own worst enemy"?
2. Which character trait is more important to develop — self-control or fearlessness?
3. Why should we fear some things? Name something or a situation that it is good to fear.

Kate's Brother Jack

"YOU SEEM TO THINK A GREAT DEAL OF YOUR SISTER," SAID one of Jack's chums to him the other day, as if the fact was rather surprising.

"Why, yes, I do," responded Jack heartily. "Kit and I are great friends."

"You always," continued the other, "seem to have such a good time when you are out together."

"Well," laughed Jack, "the fact is that when I have Kit out I keep all the while forgetting that she isn't some other fellow's sister."

I pondered somewhat over this conversation, wishing that all the brothers and sisters in the world were as good friends as Jack and Kate Hazell, and wondering why they were not. It struck me that the answer to my query was contained in Jack's last sentence. Boys don't usually treat their sisters as they would if they were "some other fellow's sisters." Jack is a shining exception. He kneels to put on Kate's overshoes as gallantly as if she were Bessie Dare, and Bessie Dare is at present Jack's ideal of all that is loveliest in girlhood. If at a party at a neighbor's, he takes Kate in to supper himself, and cares for her in all ways as an escort should; and Kate knows what to expect of him and what to do herself, and is not in dread of desertion or of being left to the tender mercies of anyone who notices her forlorn condition. And I don't wonder, when I see how nicely he treats her, that Kate declares that she would rather have her brother Jack for an escort than almost anyone else in the world.

At home, too, Jack is a pattern. Though there is a constant merry war between brother and sister, and jokes and repartees fly thick and fast, yet it is always fair cut and thrust between them, all for sport and naught for malice; the wit never degenerates into rudeness. Then, too, if Kate does anything for him her kindness is always acknowledged. Does she take the trouble to make for him his favorite rice griddle-cakes, and then stay in the kitchen to bake them herself, that they may acquire that delicate golden brown which is so dear to the taste of all who love them truly, Jack never fails to assure her that her efforts are appreciated.

Does she paint him a teacup and saucer or embroider him a hat-band, he is as delighted as possible. He does not take all these things as a matter of course. On Saturday nights he is apt to remember her by a box of candy, a bunch of flowers, or a bottle of her favorite violet perfume. Best of all he *talks* to her. He tells her his thoughts, his hopes and fears, his disappointments, and his plans for the future. In short, they are, as he said, "great friends."

Some of Jack's comrades rather envy him his good fortune in possessing so devoted a sister as Kate, and they have been heard to say frankly that they wish their sisters were as nice as Kate Hazell. If those boys would pursue the same course of action toward their sisters that Jack does toward his, they might, perhaps, be rewarded with as delightful a result; for it is by little acts of kindness and courtesy and consideration that Jack has made of his sister a friend whose love will never grow cold, whose devotion will never falter, and whose loyalty will never fail while life shall last.

⊰ FOR FURTHER THOUGHT ⊱

1. What did you think when you read about the brother who always showed kindness and courtesy to his sister?
2. How do you see people treating each other most of the time?
3. How does God tell us to treat each other (Galatians 5:13-15, 1 Peter 4:8)?

Helping at Home

WE HEAR A GOOD DEAL THESE DAYS ABOUT BOYS BEING neglected, unappreciated individuals. It is said that everyone is so absorbed in the girls that the boys are treated rather carelessly. Some people even go so far as to say that the boys' own mothers prefer their sisters to them. If this were true it would be very dreadful. I have looked into the subject somewhat and have come to the conclusion that where such is the case it is the boys' own fault. When the sons are as attentive and helpful and loving as the daughters, their mothers usually value them about alike.

Some boys have the idea that they can't and won't do "girls' work." If those same boys would practice that sort of employment a little when mother is laid up with a sick headache, or sister Maggie is off for a well-earned week's holiday, it would be a very nice thing for the family. I know boys who have tried it and have not found it so distressing.

I have the honor to know one boy, seventeen years old, who does all the family washing every Saturday morning. His mother's only assistant in her housework is his little sister, aged ten, and the son has decided that during his school life there is one burden that he can take from his mother's weary shoulders, and that is the great bugbear of washing day; and so every Saturday morning he rolls his shirt sleeves up to his shoulders, ties a good stout apron in front of him, and plunges into the suds; and it is one of the most beautiful sights I know of to see him "Cheerily rub and rinse and wring and hang up the clothes to dry."

I know another boy who did all of his family's ironing during one summer, except the shirts: those, he was forced to confess, were too much for his skill. I know boys who can run the sewing machine, and who can sweep, wash dishes, and trim lamps on occasion. I even know boys who can cook. One boy in particular I call to mind whose corn muffins are the pride of the family, and if there is company Jim is always called upon to contribute some of his inimitable hot corn-cakes for breakfast. These boys, I assure you, are appreciated in the home circle; and when their mothers talk them over, if their right ears don't burn, why, there's no truth in signs, that's all!

If there is no need for a boy to do housework, then let him do whatever is his appointed work with cheerful promptness. Every boy ought to have, and most boys do have, some daily tasks to do, the non-performance of which makes a jar in the family machine. If you have the furnace fire in charge, see to it regularly night and morning. I know a boy whose work it is to take care of the furnace in his home, and he could hardly seem more unwilling to go down the cellar stairs if that cellar was a dungeon cell in which he was about to be incarcerated for life.

His father, his mother, and his sisters all have to "be after" him twice a day in order to get him to perform that simple duty. If you have the kindling-wood to cut, keep the woodbox full. If you have an errand to do, do it pleasantly. I heard a mother request her son to go on an errand the other day, and this was the response she received: "Well, there's one thing Job didn't have to do anyhow; he didn't have to go to the store to get a quart of molasses!" There is a way of doing even an errand "heartily, as unto the Lord," and a beautiful way it is, but that boy didn't practice it that time.

Perhaps some boy who has read thus far in this article feels like reminding the writer of the old proverb, "All work and no play makes Jack a dull boy." Should that be the case, I will say that I heartily agree with the proverb, and I suggest that sometimes when "Jack" goes out to play he should take his mother with him. Astonish her by an invitation to a concert or a lecture or some other entertainment which you think she would enjoy. Devote yourself to her in your very best style for the evening and see if she does not seem pleased. If there is likely to be a good match for your baseball game or a race for your rowing club, invite your mother to witness the contest, and if your side wins she will be a proud mother.

There is a phrase which happy mothers sometimes use that has always seemed a beautiful one to me, because when I hear it I know that the one of whom it is spoken is strong and gentle, thoughtful, helpful, and cheery; in short, much that a son ought to be. And I hope that the mother of every boy who reads these lines can say of him fondly and proudly, "He is a good son; he is his 'mother's own boy.'"

⊰ FOR FURTHER THOUGHT ⊱

1. What does the phrase "Mother's own boy" mean?
2. What kinds of things could you do for your mom (and for the whole family) to deserve that praise?
3. How could you help your mom today?

Out-of-Door Behavior

THE OTHER EVENING ROB WAS LYING ON THE SOFA IN THE library and telling me about what he called a "little adventure" which he had had a day or two before. He had met a young girl on the ferry-boat whom he had never seen before, and, as he expressed it, "had had some fun with her."

"Why, Rob," said I, "you don't mean to say that you have been flirting, and with a young lady who was a total stranger to you beside!"

"Well," he answered, laughing a little, "she wasn't exactly a *young lady*, you know. But that is just what I did."

"I am sorry to hear it," said I.

"Where is the harm?" he answered. "She liked it. I would not have done it if she hadn't."

"That is just it," I responded, "and if you had not done it, certainly she could not, for it always takes two to make a flirtation as well as a bargain."

"Seems to me," said Rob, sitting up and looking at me, "seems to me you are taking a little bit of nonsense very seriously."

"Yes," I answered, "I am serious, but it is because I do not think it is nonsense. See here, Rob, how would you like to have someone flirt with your sisters?"

"I'd like to see any fellow try it!" was the instant response. "I'd punch his head for him. But then no fellow ever would, you know, for my sisters are ladies."

"But you should treat other fellows' sisters with the same respect which you wish them to show to your sisters," said I, applying the Golden Rule with a little twist to suit the occasion. "You ought to treat every woman, young or old, rich or poor, plain or pretty, and of whatever condition, with as much respect as if she were a lady; and you ought to do it for your own sake as well as for theirs, because it is a fact that the man or boy who habitually thinks of women disrespectfully or lightly greatly injures the tone of his moral character and opens the door to temptations which, if he yields to them, will ruin his life."

It is very pleasant for a lady to feel whenever she goes out that, as the old song says,

"Friends in all the old she'll find,
And brothers in the young."

And I am glad to say that such is the treatment which
a lady usually receives in this country. She can rely
upon a ready courtesy and a generous help, when
needed, from any man wherever she may go; and such
attentions it is pleasant to give and equally pleasant to
take.

Forever to be remembered is a certain gentleman
in rather a shabby coat and a shocking bad hat who
one rainy day was riding uptown in a Fourth Avenue
car, and who, when a young girl with her arms full of
parcels was about to get out at Denning's, stopped the
car for her, seized her umbrella, opened it, and
escorted her to the shop-door safe and dry, and then
responding to her grateful "Thank you, sir," with a
touch of the hat and a smile, ran after his car, caught
it, and disappeared therein. Equally unforgotten is
another gentleman who, when a Broadway stage
stopped in a mud puddle which the same young girl
was about to step despairingly into, said frankly, "Wait
a minute. Step on my foot and I'll swing you across,"
and suiting the action to the word, he planted his foot
in what was apparently the worst spot of all, and as she
stepped upon it with one deft swing she was landed
safely on the opposite pavement; and she went on her
way with a thankful heart and visions of Sir Walter
Raleigh flitting through her brain.

My paper has been occupied so far with suggestions as to how you should behave to other boys' sisters; but now how shall you behave when you meet their maiden aunts, their mothers, and their grandmothers? I asked my particular Sir Philip Sydney a question once which I think throws some light on this point. I will explain that Sir Philip is a clerk in a wholesale hardware store where they have very long hours and very hard work. Said I, "Phil, do you *always* give up your seat to a lady if she is standing?"

"Well," he answered, "some nights when I am awfully tired I don't give up my seat to a young lady; but I can't bear to see an old woman, no matter whether she is a lady or not, stand while I sit."

Those whose behavior is regulated by such a spirit will always be truly courteous to their elders. It is a shame to see half a dozen young fellows spring eagerly up to give a seat to a beautiful girl, when they will not stir for a worn, faded woman, with perhaps a bundle of cheap sewing in her arms, and who is not in any case one-tenth part as able to stand as the bright, healthy young lady. They agitated the question a while ago in dear old Boston whether, if every seat in the street-car was taken and a young man should see his mother's cook enter, he was in courtesy bound—remembering that she was a woman as well as a cook—to rise and give her his seat. I for one do not see why he should not.

After all, the truest guide to a courteous behavior

is the promptings of a kindly and thoughtful spirit, and the best rule for the government of manners is the golden one. And if our boys will cultivate the one and be guided by the other, they cannot go far astray.

⊰ FOR FURTHER THOUGHT ⊱

1. What is the Golden Rule? (*Hint:* "Do unto others as you would have . . . do unto. . . .")
2. Think of at least three times someone has done something for you that made you feel cared for. What did he or she do?
3. What could you do for someone today to make him or her feel the same way?

A Talk to Shy Boys

ONE OF MY BOY FRIENDS CAME TO SEE ME A WHILE AGO; A VERY little boy he is, only six years old, but he said something which set me thinking. He is such a shy little fellow that he reminds me of nothing so much as a little turtle shut up in his shell. When he is alone with me, however, he sometimes opens his shell and gives me a glimpse of what is going on inside. He did so on this occasion. He was seated on the edge of the big rocking chair with his small hands thrust into the pockets of his first knickerbockers. His brow was wrinkled and he looked very unhappy. Being such a little fellow, he could not express himself with much fluency, but to me his very blunders were eloquent.

"I've got to go a-visiting," he remarked gloomily. "I've got to go with mamma to see my grandma. Do you know I have a grandma? I have, and I've got aunties—I've got uncles— and I've got—folks."

He enumerated his relations as if each particular class were an especial affliction. He continued: "There's an awful lot of people at my grandma's house." Here he left his chair and nestled close to me. "I'll tell you something," he said mysteriously; "I'm afraid of them. Last time I went there I shivered—I didn't say anything, but I shivered."

And I thought of dozens of boys whom I know, who are a good deal older than my little turtle, to whom the hours which they are forced to spend in society are so many hours of silent agony. Like little Jack, they don't say anything, but they shiver.

A while ago, too, I was present at an examination in one of the most thorough private schools in the city. When the class in French conversation was examined, two brothers whom I knew were in it. The elder was the more thorough French scholar of the two, but the younger carried off the honors solely on account of his superior coolness and composure. He was quite ready to chat with his teacher, and even made a bright little joke in French which delighted his audience. But when it was his brother's turn, every idea forsook him;

he started, flushed, and could only stammer out, "*J'oublie, Monsieur*" (I forget, sir), and sat covered with confusion as with a garment.

"I knew how it would be," he said, hopelessly, afterwards. "I always go to pieces during oral examinations."

I felt so sorry for Hal that when I went home I told Mrs. Experience about it. Mrs. Experience is a wise woman who lives in our family and whom I often consult on my own and other people's difficulties.

"I wish," said I to her, "that I could do something to help shy boys."

"I will tell you a little story that perhaps may assist you," she said, smiling.

"When I taught school twenty years ago in Wisconsin, I had a scholar named Sam B—. He was eighteen years old and was exceedingly tall and awkward. He was backward in his studies, for his educational advantages had been limited; but he was very conscious of his defects and feared ridicule. I think he was the most bashful fellow I have ever known. Notwithstanding all this he was bent on gaining an education and was determined, as he expressed it, to 'make a man of himself.'

"Of course I was ready to help him, and as he had a fine mind, he went forward rapidly in his studies.

"Now it was a rule of mine that my pupils should each prepare either a declamation or a composition for every Friday. This rule Sam had hitherto been excused from. When I thought him sufficiently advanced, however, I told him to be prepared with a declamation on the following Friday.

"'Oh! Miss Grace,' he objected, 'I can't; anything but that! I never could speak a piece. All the fellows would laugh at the very idea.'

"'But, Sam,' I urged, 'it will be the best thing in the world for you. What you lack is confidence in yourself, and that would help you to gain it.'

"'I should certainly fail,' he answered.

"'Sam,' said I, 'you won't fail if you make up your mind to succeed. At all events you must recite some selection before the school on Friday next.'

"'What will you do if I refuse?' asked he.

"'You would be obliged to leave the school,' I answered promptly. 'I can have no scholar in my school who refuses to accede to my wishes.'

"'Well,' he replied, 'that's fair. If I make up my mind that I can't speak, of course I'll leave.'

"I watched for Friday with a good deal of anxiety. In about the middle of the exercises I said, 'We will now have a recitation by Samuel B—.'

"Sam turned all sorts of colors, but he walked forward to the platform, made his bow, and essayed to speak; but he shook all over and the words would not come. Fifty pairs of curious eyes seemed to bore into his very soul, and his voice died away in a husky whisper. He walked stiffly to the water-pail, took a drink, and came back to the platform; just then he heard a suppressed titter, and that struck fire. Grasping a shaking knee in each hand, he thus apostrophized his recreant limbs:

"'Keep still,' he cried, 'keep still, I tell you, for I *will* speak.'

"That loosed his tongue, and the famous old periods came rolling out:

"'Not many generations ago, where we now sit, encircled by all that exalts and embellishes civilized life, the rank thistle nodded in the wind and the wild fox dug his hole unscared,' and so on.

"That boy," concluded Mrs. Experience, fanning herself complacently, "became a member of Congress from his native State, and a very eloquent speaker he is too."

I thanked Mrs. Experience for her kindness in telling me this story and went on thinking, but it seemed to me that I saw a glimmer of daylight.

That very evening Charlie Axtell dropped into the sitting-room, just home from his first trip West as a commercial traveler. Now Charlie is a very domestic, home-loving fellow, modest and unobtrusive, with but a small opinion of himself, and such being the case, I feared he had not enjoyed his Western experiences very much.

"Oh!" said he, in answer to my questions, "at the start it was awful. I walked up and down in front of my first customer's door for fully half an hour without the courage to go in, and when I did get into the store I hadn't a word to say for myself and precious few for my firm. How I did it I don't know, but I managed to make a small sale, so my first effort was not an absolute failure; but the first two weeks were terrifying. I wasn't going to let myself be beaten, though, so I persevered, and take it all in all, I have made a very successful trip."

One little sentence of Charlie's stuck in my head. *"I wasn't going to let myself be beaten,"* he said. Ah! that was it. The boy who is deterred from doing anything by shyness lets himself be beaten. His shyness conquers him when he should conquer the shyness.

One of our most noted humorous lecturers once asked Mr. Beecher what he should do to overcome a certain nervous trembling which always attacked him whenever he faced an audience.

"My boy," said the wise old veteran, "I don't think that you will ever get over it; *you had best not mind it*."

This habit of shyness, if nursed and yielded to, may come to dominate a man's whole life, and may so fetter his actions that half his native powers may never be fully developed; but if fought with it can be conquered and put down and kept in its proper place. Sam did it when he resolved that he *would* speak. Charlie did it when he determined not to be beaten, and every boy can do so if he will exert his own courage and self-control.

⊰ FOR FURTHER THOUGHT ⊱

1. What is the scariest thing you've ever had to do in front of other people?

2. What goes through your mind—what do you think will happen—when you become the center of attention?
3. If you're not a shy person, what advice could you give to encourage someone to get past his shyness?

A Talk to Awkward Boys

THERE IS A TIME IN THE LIFE OF MANY A LAD WHEN DURING the course of a year, or perhaps even a shorter period, he changes from a little fellow into a big boy. It is marvelous how fast he grows; before his friends know it he is taller than his father. He has to have as many new suits as a silk worm does to keep him looking respectable, and in spite of every care there is apt to be a gap between the bottoms of his trousers and the tops of his shoes, and a wide strip of wrist between his sleeves and his hands. Sometimes they call this season the "awkward age," and a very hard time it often is to a lad; many are the jokes that are cracked at his expense, and in some families many are the sighs and critical remarks which he hears about his looks, his carriage, or behavior, from friends who ought to know better; while the poor boy himself feels more than anyone else can feel that his feet and hands are more than he can manage, and that when he sits down he seems to have as many joints as a grasshopper, and he always appears to himself to be ten times more clumsy and awkward than he does to anyone else.

I number more than one such boy among my friends, and the other day one of them was telling me how queer and shy he felt, just like dear Hans Andersen's ugly duckling—how he never could bear to get into company because he did not know what to do or say; and one would think, to hear the boy talk, that life under the circumstances was scarcely worth living.

"Why, Herbert," said I, "have a little patience with yourself; in time that tall frame of yours will fill out and assume its proper proportions and you will learn how to govern it; its muscles will knit if you give them sufficient exercise. The lines of your face will change, and by the time you are twenty-five years old you will probably be a man of fine appearance, and, if you will take the pains to cultivate them, of easy and graceful manners."

"But," said the young Hopeless, "suppose I shouldn't turn out as you think I will? Suppose I keep on looking awkward and queer to the end of the chapter?"

"Why, then," said I still cheerfully, "listen to this: I have a friend who when he was a lad was certainly the most awkward and angular boy that I ever saw. His face was plain to the verge of ugliness; he stammered so badly that it was only by speaking with the most painful slowness and precision he was able to control his speech so as to make himself understood, and he

had absolutely but two good points about him: one was
a nobly shaped head, and the other was a gentle and
agreeable tone of voice. In spite of all of these draw-
backs, he has not only won a most enviable rank
among the scientists of this country, but he is distinguished for his beautiful manners as well. He has
learned to behave so charmingly, and with such uncon-
sciousness of self, that people forget his looks when
they have been in his company ten minutes, and only
notice the rare and noble attributes of mind and character which he possesses. As he grew older he learned
to manage himself better, and he became accustomed
to his own peculiarities, so to speak; for though they
were toned down somewhat as he reached manhood,
they never left him, but he bears with them so pleasantly himself that to his friends they are actually an
added charm. He never alludes to them in any way,
excepting that I have heard him make to strangers a
winning little apology for his manner of speech, which
is still very slow, though his utterance is easy. But
though his speech is slow, his thoughts are quick, and
he is always thoughtful for others. He has a beautiful
deference in his manners toward his elders, no lady is
ever near him that she does not feel a sense of his quiet
consideration for her, and all children turn naturally
to him for protection and care; and his brilliant mind
and beautiful spirit together have so dignified and
ennobled the body which they inhabit that everyone
who knows him regards him with admiration, respect,

and affection. It is the finest example of the triumph of mind over matter that I have ever seen."

A mere awkwardness is almost always outgrown, or, if it does not entirely vanish with maturity, it ceases to annoy unless its cause springs from some physical defect which time cannot cure. Some boys perhaps, who chance to be reading this, may have the lot to go through life crippled or maimed, not equal physically in some way to their comrades. To such I would say with great gentleness and sympathy, be careful not to let any over-sensitiveness keep you back or prevent you from taking your share of work or play whenever you can; and cultivate steadily the habit of forgetting yourself and entering heartily into the hopes and pursuits of others. For it is a fact that a physical peculiarity or defect, if its owner allows it to trouble him, can mar or even ruin the usefulness and happiness of a life; but if it is bravely and cheerfully borne it never fails to give a peculiar nobility to the spirit of the one who so takes it.

And not only that, but such a defect may be overcome, and in spite of it one may do such good and manly work in the world that those who are in the perfect possession of all their faculties must pause in admiration of the man who, though so hindered, accomplishes such beautiful results.

When the late William Fawcett, of England, was a young man of eighteen, he was out shooting, and his eyesight was destroyed by the accidental discharge of a gun which was in the hands of his father. The agony of the poor father when he found, after weeks of suspense, that his dear son was hopelessly blind, was almost unendurable, and the brave boy to comfort him said, "Father, don't grieve so. I promise you that this accident shall not ruin my life. Everything that I had planned to do before it happened I will accomplish still. You shall see."

As soon as he was able he returned to college and took his degree. Then he came home and practiced vigorously all sorts of manly exercises, even to riding horseback—a pastime in which he delighted as long as he lived. When his not overly firm health was fully restored he began to consider what he could best do to help his fellow-men; he turned his attention to politics, and was elected to Parliament, and for many years his name was identified with every needed reform and with all legislation which was for his country's good. Finally he was made Postmaster General of England, and he filled that high office to the satisfaction of the whole country, and when he died, a few years since, England mourned him as one of her best and bravest sons. And the man who did all this was perfectly blind.

So, my boy to whom God has thought best to send some similar affliction, never repine, never despair; but remember that with God to help you, and your own determined will, there is no limit to the things which you may accomplish if you try.

❧ FOR FURTHER THOUGHT ❦

1. What kinds of messages do you get from television, movies, and magazines about physical appearance? Are the messages true or false?
2. Can you think of at least one reason why we should be less concerned with the physical part of ourselves than the mental and spiritual parts?

On Teasing

IT SEEMS TO ME THAT ONE OF THE MOST ANNOYING TRAITS OF character one can possess is a disposition to tease, for when that disposition is freely indulged there is nothing that can cause more unhappiness to others. To be obliged to spend one's life with an inveterate tease is like living in a bramble bush, or suffering constantly from the torture of innumerable pin-pricks. To be sure, one pin-prick is nothing much, but when one has to bear ten thousand of them it is quite another matter.

"Pshaw!" says the tease, "I did not hurt you any. I wouldn't make such a fuss about nothing. I did not *mean* anything. I was only teasing."

Exactly. And it is just because there is no meaning in it nor necessity for it, because it is "only teasing," that poor tormented, insulted human nature cries out sometimes in a passion against it. It is astonishing what an unerring ingenuity a born tease will show in choosing his victim's weakest point and in sticking his little pin straight into it. Is his victim timid, quick-tempered, or has he some infirmity of speech or peculiarity of person about which he is sensitive? That is the very place which the tease selects for his thrust; and a tease never misses a chance. If he cannot find anything else to annoy, he will tease an animal or torment a little child, and he thinks it is fun; but it is the most malicious, most dreadful, and most dangerous fun in this world.

I once knew a lady who was literally almost frightened to death by a miserable man who followed her home through the twilight; she reached shelter and dropped fainting upon the floor, and the thoughtless fellow who occasioned the distress explained that he "just followed her to tease her, because he knew she was timid, and he did it just for fun." He found that it was not so enjoyable as he waited while she hovered between life and death, the victim of his wretched joke. Fortunately for him and for the friends who loved her, she recovered, but she never entirely got over the effects of the nervous shock which she endured at that time.

I think that a genuine tease is always a coward, for he never attacks his equals: his victims are the helpless animal, the little child, the timid woman. If you will notice, it is never the smaller boy who teases the larger one. And then a tease can never bear to be teased himself. Nothing makes him angrier than to be paid back in his own coin.

But really, the most distressing thing about the

whole matter is the effect which the habit of teasing has upon the nature of the one who indulges in it. A confirmed tease becomes positively heartless. He can look upon mental or physical distress quite unmoved. Indeed, he is not satisfied with the results of his teasing if he does not cause one or the other. That is the part he enjoys, and it is why he teases.

If there is a boy who reads these lines who likes to tease his little sister until she runs in tears to her mother, or who torments some little fellow at school just to see him flush crimson and bristle with impotent indignation—if you want to make a man of yourself, stop it. For it is a most ignoble and unmanly thing to take delight in causing pain to any living creature, especially if it is smaller and weaker than yourself.

⊰FOR FURTHER THOUGHT⊱

1. What's the difference between good teasing and bad teasing?
2. What can happen to a person if he gets in the habit of teasing others?

On Being Pleasant

SAYS MR. THACKERAY ABOUT THAT NICE BOY CLIVE NEWCOME, "I don't know that Clive was especially brilliant, but he was *pleasant*."

Occasionally we meet people to whom it seems to come naturally to be pleasant; such are as welcome wherever they go as flowers in May, and the most charming thing about them is that they help to make other people pleasant too. Their pleasantness is contagious.

The other morning we were in the midst of a three days' rain. The fire smoked, the dining room was chilly, and when we assembled for breakfast, Papa looked rather grim and Mamma tired, for the baby had been restless all night. Polly was plainly inclined to fretfulness, and Bridget was undeniably cross, when Jack came in with the breakfast rolls from the baker's. He had taken off his rubber coat and boots in the entry, and he came in rosy and smiling.

"Here's the paper, sir," said he to his father with such a cheerful tone that his father's brow relaxed, and he said, "Ah, Jack, thank you," quite pleasantly.

His mother looked up at him smiling, and he just touched her cheek gently as he passed.

"The top of the morning to you, Pollywog," he said to his little sister, and delivered the rolls to Bridget with a "Here you are, Bridget. Aren't you sorry you didn't go to get them yourself this beautiful day?"

He gave the fire a poke and opened a damper. The smoke ceased, and presently the coals began to glow, and five minutes after Jack came in we had gathered around the table and were eating our oatmeal as cheerily as possible. This seems very simple in the telling, and Jack never knew he had done anything at all, but he had in fact changed the whole moral atmosphere of the room and had started a gloomy day pleasantly for five people.

"He is always so," said his mother, when I spoke to her about it afterwards, "just so sunny and kind all the time. I suppose there are more brilliant boys in the world than mine, but none with a kinder heart or a sweeter temper; I am sure of that."

And I thought, "Why isn't such a disposition worth cultivating? Isn't it one's duty to be pleasant, just as well as to be honest or truthful, or industrious or generous? And yet, while there are a good many honest, truthful, industrious, and generous souls in the world, and people who are unselfish too after a fashion, a person who is habitually pleasant is rather a rarity. I suppose the reason is because it is such hard work to act pleasant when one feels cross."

People whose dispositions are naturally irritable or unhappy think it is no use trying to be otherwise; but that is a mistake. Any one can be pleasant who wants to. If one will patiently and perseveringly try to keep always pleasant, after a while one will get in the habit of smiling instead of frowning, of looking bright instead of surly, and of giving a kind word instead of a cross one. And if some of the boys who read this should chance to be of the kind who only act pleasant when they feel like it, I wish they would think of what I say, and try and see if I am not right. And the beauty of it is, as I said before, that pleasantness is catching, and before long they may find themselves in the midst of a circle full of bright and happy people, where everyone is as good-natured and contented as they are.

⊰ FOR FURTHER THOUGHT ⊱

1. What does the author say is the most contagious character quality?
2. What is the best "heart" medicine in the world? (Read Proverbs 15:13,15,30; 17:22.)

On Laughing

Jog on, jog on, the foot-path way,
And merrily hent [leap over] the stile-a;
A merry heart goes all the day,
Your sad tires in a mile-a.

SHAKESPEARE

THERE IS NO MORE DELIGHTFUL SOUND ON EARTH THAN A hearty laugh. One good laugh will brighten the whole day for the laugher and cheer everybody within hearing. But every laugh is not like that. Some laughs hurt instead of help, and their sting remains long after the careless laugher has gone on his way and forgotten what he was laughing at. I think that is what the Bible means when it gives the kindly warning that there is a *time* to laugh.

Some time since, five of my boy friends were

appointed to a committee to select the subjects for the coming quarter for the young people's prayer-meeting of their church. Four of the boys were the sons of well-to-do parents. They had plenty of money and good clothes, they were well-bred, well-educated, and altogether delightful young fellows. The fifth was a lad who had been born and brought up under very different circumstances. Fatherless, motherless, uneducated, and poor, he had struggled for existence from his babyhood, but through all his troubles he had kept an honest and cheerful heart. Naturally intelligent, he was always learning, and all the boys of the Street Church liked and respected Joe. On the appointed evening the committee met at the house of one of the lads where I was making a visit. They went into the library and held their meeting, and after an hour or so I heard them out in the hall having the last words and giving cordial hand-shakes and good-byes to Joe, who was obliged to leave early. The hall door closed and there was an instant's silence; then the four boys who were left came leap-frogging across the hall and into the dining-room where I was sitting, and dropping on the floor around my sofa, they all went off into peals of long-suppressed laughter. After a while they managed to control themselves and tell me the joke. It seemed that Joe had mispronounced a word in a peculiarly funny manner, and the way in which he applied it made it sound supremely ridiculous to the fun-loving lads who were listening; but not one of them smiled in the slightest, or even moved a muscle, lest Joe should notice and his feelings should be hurt. They controlled themselves perfectly until Joe had gone, and then nature was too much for them and they laughed till they cried, when it could do no harm. They never repeated the story to any of their mates, so that Joe's feelings were carefully guarded in every way, and he never knew that he had said anything unusual or absurd. And I thought to myself that the Master whom those boys were serving must have been well pleased at such an instance of their thoughtfulness and self-control.

Never laugh at a jest on a sacred subject, even though the temptation may be strong. All such jesting is a species of profanity, and the influence of every boy who is trying to do right should be against it.

There are a great many practical jokes which do not deserve to be laughed at. Anything which causes inconvenience or pain to another is brutal and cannot by any possibility be amusing.

Never laugh at a vulgar joke. But laugh at a joke on yourself even if it is a little severe, for it is the best sort of practice. Many people can be very witty at other people's expense, who do not like the laugh to be turned on them. It is a good rule never to give a joke that you would not like to take.

But of honest, wholesome, hearty laughter this world can never have too much; so cultivate a merry heart which is brave enough to laugh at the little cares and annoyances of life, and you will find every day plenty of things both lighthearted and sweet to gladden you. This is the kind of heart which the Bible says "does good like a medicine." It is such a heart that Shakespeare meant when he wrote the jolly little song which I have put at the head of this article, and it is the kind of heart which everybody loves and always has loved since the world began. And if you have such a heart you will brighten the "foot-path" way of everyone whom you meet as you travel on life's journey.

⊰ FOR FURTHER THOUGHT ⊱

1. Laughter has been referred to as "internal jogging." It's a wonderful gift to be able to see the humor in life and make others laugh. However, the author talks about three kinds of jokes that are never appropriate. What are the three kinds of jokes? Why are they inappropriate?
2. Why do you think your parents are concerned with the books and magazines you read and the movies you watch?

Missions for Boys

THE WORD *MISSION* COMES FROM THE OLD LATIN VERB *MITTO*, "to send," so that a missionary is one who is sent. In these days there are a great many missions, both home and foreign, and thousands of people are working in them, preaching to and teaching and helping in many different ways the poor, the lonely, the ignorant, and the oppressed. But boys, as a general rule, do not do very much missionary work. I do not think this is their fault, however, for boys have naturally just as much of a missionary spirit as anyone else. But the trouble is they have not "been sent." And boys can give such valuable help if they will that I feel like "sending" every boy I know and giving them a hint or two as to how to begin; and perhaps I can do that best by telling how some of my boy friends have been working recently.

Not very long ago, in a Consumptives' Home, which I sometimes visit, a boy of nineteen was dying. Week by week life was slipping away from him, and one by one all the bright hopes of his youth and young manhood were departing. He was a lad who had looked poverty in the face since he was a little child. He had never known in all his life what it was to be thoroughly well clothed and fed. While but a child he had been obliged to work, and his scanty wages had always been cheerfully divided with his mother and little sisters; and then, just as the future began to grow brighter before him, the effect of his long years of toil and privation was made manifest and he was stricken with consumption.

Friends procured for him a pleasant and sunny room at the "Home," where, surrounded by every comfort, he was free and welcome to remain as long as he lived. At first the peace and quiet of his little room, the rest and freedom from anxiety, were all he craved. But afterward, when the excellent nursing which he received and the nourishing food which he ate began to tell upon his exhausted system, and he began to revive, he missed his former busy life and his old friends and companions desperately. He missed their boyish talk, their fun and laughter above all. This quiet, monotonous life was something he was utterly unused to, and he became very lonely. The ladies who managed the Home came often to see him, and he was very grateful to them and learned to love them. His mother and sisters came, sorrowful and anxious, so their visits could not cheer him, and as he said to his Sunday school teacher, he wanted "the boys." So she told his old class about it, and they agreed, as they expressed it, "to stand by Frank as long as he lived." So they went to see him regularly every visiting day in turn and spent every Sunday morning with him besides. They were all working boys, and it was sometimes a real sacrifice for them to spend the scanty time they had for recreation with Frank, but they never missed [spending time with] him once for nearly a year.

They soon discovered that Frank did not care to talk about his sufferings, but that he did like very much to know all about their plans, their work and play, and all the details of that dear everyday life which he had left forever behind him; so they talked to him about what they were doing, and many a hearty laugh rang out from Frank's room at the relation of some droll anecdote or bit of nonsense from one of the boys.

On Sunday mornings they always used to go over the Sunday school lesson together, and then they would read aloud from some good paper.

These boys kept, beside their regular envelope for Sunday collections, a horn tipped with silver which had this inscription around its edge: "Once I was the horn of an ox, I am a missionary box." And in this they used to take up collections for whatever object they chose. During Frank's illness he had frequent presents which were bought with this money. Rather amusing were some of the purchases, too, and yet, as Frank said, they each went to the spot.

Toward the last Frank could only see his kind friends for a few minutes at a time; they used to go in and sit quietly by his bed, and when they left they would give his hand a gentle clasp and say warmly, "Keep up your courage, old boy," or "Don't give in; we fellows remember you in class prayer-meeting every time." And so, helped and encouraged by his friends, Frank passed through the dark valley, brave and faithful to the last, and reached his home in that happy country whose inhabitants never say, "I am sick."

I know another class of boys who are interested in a poor woman who has a sick husband and six little daughters to provide for. These boys are sons of parents in good circumstances, and many are the glasses of soda-water and pounds of candy which they deny themselves for the sake of "their little girls," as they call them; and frequently on a Saturday before they are out on their bicycles or off for a game of some sort, one or another will go bounding up the four flights of stairs which lead to the tenement where their protégés live, with a special gift for a special little pet.

I know another set of boys who live in the country, and they collect every season crates of delicious fruit—grapes, apples, peaches, and pears—and send them to the poor children in the city. This deserves a story by itself, as I well know, for I sometimes help to distribute the gift, and I can never forget the look of the eager little mouths which are reached up to take it—mouths, sometimes, which have not tasted one single bit of fresh fruit all during the long hot summer.

My dear boys, I think I have told you enough to give you a hint of how to begin being missionaries. You have only to look about you, and you will find somebody to whom you can lend a helping hand. But if you should fail to find an opening for yourself, just go to your pastor or teacher, and he will soon put you on the track of somebody; and when you have once begun I don't think you will ever care to stop, for the great beauty of all such work is that it ennobles the nature of the one who helps as well as comforts and encourages the one who is in need, for as Mr. Lowell so beautifully says,

"Who shares his bread with a beggar feeds three,
Himself, his suffering neighbor, and Me."

Which is only another way of saying, "Inasmuch as ye

have done it unto one of the least of these ye have done it unto Me."

And I trust there is not a single boy who reads these words who would not run with eagerness to do a kindness to his Lord and Savior.

⊰ FOR FURTHER THOUGHT ⊱

1. What is a missionary?
2. When you help others, who also benefits from what you do?
3. What do Proverbs 14:31, Matthew 25:40, and Hebrews 6:10 tell us about how God views acts of kindness and compassion toward others?

On Being a Gentleman

WHAT IS IT TO BE A GENTLEMAN? IF YOU ASK MR. WEBSTER, he will tell you that any man who is well-educated, polite, and civil ranks in this country as a gentleman. But I think that today most people acknowledge that it takes more than that to make a gentleman.

"It takes blue blood," says Charlie. I suppose Charlie means by that expression that to be a gentleman a man must come of a noble and distinguished ancestry; but I have known many a man who came of a noble race who was not truly a gentleman. Though an honorable ancestry is a thing to thank God for and to be glad of, yet that in itself is not necessary to make a gentleman, for a man may have been born in a poorhouse and know nothing about his father and mother, and yet be a gentleman. Look a little deeper. What does the word *gentle* mean? To be gentle, says Mr. Webster, is never to be rough, harsh, or severe. So then, a gentleman must have polite manners and never be rough, harsh, or severe. But to be a thorough gentleman takes more than this.

A short time since, an American visiting London for the first time was invited to a reception to meet a very distinguished company. During the evening he found himself seated beside a pleasant-looking gentleman; they entered into conversation and the American told his neighbor that he was from the United States, and that it was his first evening out in London.

"Indeed," said the other, smiling. "And how do you like us?"

"Oh," was the hearty response, "I like you all greatly. Everybody is very kind; but, to tell you the truth, I think your titles very confusing. I find that I am getting my dukes and earls all mixed up, and I am afraid that I don't address anyone properly."

His neighbor's eyes sparkled. "Ah," said he, "in America you don't have that trouble."

"Oh, no," was the answer. "There any man is a gentleman who tells the truth and pays his debts, and we are all plain Misters."

The other looked amused, but just then a gentleman came up, and bowing profoundly, addressed the American's companion as "Your Royal Highness," and with a courteous smile and a bow, H. R. H. walked off, leaving Mr. C anxiously considering the tone of his previous remarks, and wondering if they had been too free and easy for the ears of royalty.

But the American's idea of what constituted a gentleman throws another light on the subject. A gentleman *must* pay his debts and speak the truth. He must verify the old proverb that "a gentleman's word is as good as his bond." If he passes his word he must keep it at any hazard, and every word he says must come within the limit of absolute truth. And a gentleman must live within his income. True, many a true gentleman has known poverty's bitterest sting, and has seen his property melt away from him like snowflakes in springtime, leaving him positively penniless; then it is right to take help from others, both for one's self and for one's family. But such help is never obtained under false pretenses, and a true gentleman, if he is ever able, will repay the donors.

So, then, a gentleman must be polite, gentle, truthful, and honest. And if a boy wishes to become a gentleman, and will rule his life by those four words, he will succeed. But he will find when he begins to try that those four words, simple as they are, have deep meanings, and it may not be always easy for him to put them into daily practice. But if he wishes an example by which to mold his life, I can point him to one perfect model, Jesus Christ, who was, as the poet truly says, "The first of gentlemen."

Never before or since have there been shown in this world such beautiful manners as His, so courteous, so friendly, and marked with such an unfailing tact and kindness, whether they addressed the young, the middle-aged, or the old.

And was not He the very essence of gentleness?— a gentleness which had no trace of weakness in it, but rather one that was born of conscious power and perfect self-control.

And who but He could say that He was Truth itself?

And though He was born, and lived and died, in poverty, yet no one of all His enemies, and He had many eager to find some flaw, could point to the slightest stain on His integrity and honor.

A lad who hopes to win this high ideal must make up his mind to spend his life in trying; but it will pay him, for he will find sooner or later that in aiming to be a gentleman he is only trying to make himself like Christ.

⚔ FOR FURTHER THOUGHT ⚔

1. Most people use the word *gentleman* as a synonym for male person. But what qualities does a boy or man need to possess to be a true gentleman?

2. Why does the author say that "aiming to be a gentleman" is the same as becoming like Christ?

When "Tomorrow" Comes

"YOU WILL BE SURE TO LIKE HIM," SAID DICK. "EVERYBODY does."

Dick was speaking of one of his college chums whom he was going to bring to call the next day.

"What is his specialty?" I asked. "Does he 'go in' for athletics or study or society? Is he musical or dramatic? or is he noted for anything in particular?"

"Oh no," answered Dick, "Frank is not noted for anything in special. Stop," said he laughing, "I am wrong. He *is* noted for having the best rat-terrier in college: his name is Snap, and one day"—but the prowess of that particular little dog does not belong to this story.

The next afternoon while we were all out on the piazza Dick brought Frank over and introduced him, and I did like him. I liked him at first glance. He had such an active, well-knit, graceful figure, such merry black eyes, and such a fun-loving mouth. He sat down upon the piazza step and began to talk as if he had known us all his life; it was a pleasant, breezy sort of chat, such as any one would like to listen to. There were bits from the football field and the boatclub in it; there was the last undergraduate joke and a snatch of the latest college song hummed in a very good tenor, and there were anecdotes of Snap the valiant.

We learned to know Frank very well that summer;

he was always coming over to play tennis with the girls, or to drink lemonade under the copper beech, or to lounge in the hammock, and he was always the merriest and best-natured companion imaginable, but he was never anything more. We found before long that his father had chosen our quiet village for Frank's summer home in order to keep him, as that young man himself expressed it, "out of harm's way."

One day he came in and seated himself in a big Shaker chair near my work-table.

"What makes you look so serious?" he asked.

"Do you never feel a little serious?" was my counter-question.

"Never," he answered. "Time enough to take life seriously when I am older."

"Surely," said I, "you must sometimes think of the future, and of the life-work which lies before you."

"Never," said he again, as he lifted his tennis cap, and added, smiling roguishly, "the *present* is enough for me."

"But," said I, "I am going to *make* you be serious for a little while. I am going to talk to you as if I were your aunt, or your grandmother, or something."

"Do," said he cordially: "I am all ears; don't be afraid; say anything you like."

"It seems to me," said I slowly, "that you are not getting all that you might out of your college life."

"Well," he answered reflectively, "I don't *know* any fellow who gets more pressure of fun to the square inch than I do. What more can you suggest?"

"Do you never think of anything but fun?"

"Never."

"But are you not sometimes afraid of the consequences?" I urged.

"Well," he answered, sitting up, "I will just tell you my plan. You know that at a certain college if we get a certain number of bad marks, we get a private reprimand; if we continue in the same way, we get a public reprimand; if we keep it up after that, we are expelled. So at the beginning of the year I 'just sail in' and use up all my bad marks until I get my private reprimand, then I have to sober down for the remainder of the year; but last year I went a little too far and got my public 'rep,' too, and that was rather dangerous. My father objected."

"But," said I, anxiously, "you don't do things that are really wrong, do you?"

How he laughed. "What things do you call 'really wrong,' grandmamma?" said he.

"Well," I answered, hesitatingly, "gambling, for instance. You don't do that, I am sure."

"Don't I?" said he; "I wish you would persuade my father of that. I will give you half of my next winnings for your pet charity if you will."

I gave up in despair.

"Don't fret about me, grandmamma," said Frank quickly, for he saw I was touched. "I'm only sowing my wild oats, and that is every young fellow's privilege; by-and-by I will reform: ten years from now I will be as steady as the town pump, you see if I am not."

I could only shake my head at the handsome, careless fellow and leave him to go his own way.

He was never graduated from his college. During the following year a wild escapade of his came to the knowledge of the faculty, and he was expelled. Then his father put him into business; but he had formed no habits of thrift or of industry, and he did not succeed. Shortly after that his father died, and Frank soon dissipated his patrimony, and then he was thrown upon his own resources, but he seemed unable to do anything. Situations were procured for him only for him to lose them, and in ten years time no one would have recognized in the shabby, idle, dispirited man—willing to accept a favor from anyone, living on the charity of a few old friends—the brilliant Frank of other years.

A short time after and the sad tragedy was ended. He left no record of high achievement or of any victory won. The world was no better for his having lived in it, and at the end of the finished story of his life we only write the one sad word *failure*.

⊰For Further Thought⊱

1. How is it possible to have so much potential and be so well liked, yet be a total failure at life?
2. What's wrong with never thinking about the future?

The Thoughtless Boy

THERE IS A CERTAIN FAULT WHICH MANY PEOPLE DO NOT count as a fault at all—they speak of it as "a defect," "a blemish," "a failing," and yet that little fault injures more characters, spoils more lives, causes more unhappiness, than many another sin which we think far more dreadful. The fault of which I write is thoughtlessness, and I think that boys are rather prone to that habit: but no matter how friendly, how bright, or how obliging a boy may be—no matter how much he may mean to do right—if he is thoughtless, it spoils it all; for don't you see, if you cannot *depend* upon a boy's doing the right thing—if he fails you just at the critical moment—of what good are his good intentions? He may come to you the next day with his face full of honest grief. "I didn't think," says he. "I'm ever so sorry to have annoyed you so," and you know that he is sorry, for you count upon Jack's good heart always. But Jack's regret does not help matters at all.

"But," says Jack, "I cannot help it—honestly I cannot. Am I to blame for forgetting?"

"Yes, Jack, you are. You can exercise your memory just as well as you can any muscle of your body, and one will grow strong and serviceable with proper training just like the other."

"But I *have* tried to remember," says poor Jack, "and I can't do it."

"You have not tried hard enough," I insist. "You cannot break up that miserable habit in a day, nor a week, nor a month, but in the course of a year, if you set the whole force of your nature against it, your friends will see a decided change in you for the better.

"If you promise your mother that you will be home promptly at three to do an errand for her, be there at the minute, if you have to tie strings around every one of your ten fingers to make you remember your engagement.

"If you promise to buy a copy of the *Tribune* for your Aunt Mary on your way to school and bring it home to her when you come back, and Harry Davison joins you as he did the other day and you get so engaged in chat that you walk five blocks beyond the newsstand before you think of the paper, leave Harry Davison and go back and get it. You will have to run, and you will probably be a little late at school, so that you will have a mark for tardiness, for you will have no proper excuse. Of course your Aunt Mary would forgive you if you did not bring her the paper. True, you might buy her one on your way home from school, if they were not all sold, but do not rely upon any of these ways out of the scrape; go back as fast as you can and get the paper; if you are late at school, take your tardy mark, for you deserve it: but you will have kept your word as a gentleman should, and that is of great importance. If you treat yourself with such severity as this every time you forget anything, your memory will learn to give you the right reminder at the proper time.

"The trouble is, Jack, you do not think these things are of sufficient importance. It seems absurd to you to take all of that trouble for a newspaper, and you know that your kind aunt will accept any apology that you choose to make her. But it is not for your aunt's sake that I am writing, nor for the sake of the paper—that is a little thing; it is for the sake of your own character. It is that you may grow up to be a truthful, reliable, trust-worthy man.

"'Truthful!' you exclaim, and your color rises at that.

"Well, in one way I never knew a more truthful boy than you are. I should rely upon your account of any circumstance exactly. I know you would relate it just as it occurred. But you *said* you would mail that letter at once for me, you know—and *did* you? Yes, after it had lain all night in your breast-pocket. Of course it was only a trifle, and you were sorry, and I excused you instantly: but the ideal gentleman keeps his word in trifles, you know, as well as in things which are more important. And as it happened, that letter was not exactly a trifle, for the fact that it was not received when it should have been caused some anxiety.

"Indeed you and I never know what are the trifles of this world, for sometimes the things which appear

most trivial to our shortsighted eyes are really very serious matters; and the only way for us to live is to do
whatever comes to us in the line of duty in the most
thorough manner possible; then we shall be sure that
no trouble which could be helped will come either
to ourselves or to anyone whom we love by our
thoughtlessness."

⇥ FOR FURTHER THOUGHT ⇤

1. Why is it important to call someone if you've said
   you would . . . or meet them at the mall at a certain
   time when you've said you would meet them?
2. How do you feel when a friend makes a promise and
   doesn't keep it? What do you think the next time he
   makes you a promise?
3. How important are good intentions when it comes
   to keeping a promise? How does the idea of doing
   something only when it's convenient affect your
   character?

A Dandy

"I DO HOPE YOU WILL LIKE SAM," SAID SAM'S "BEST AUNT"
to me once, when I was going to visit at his mother's
house. "He is a very nice boy, but he has such a rough
husk that very few care to penetrate it."

Just before tea on the day I arrived at Sam's mother's we were all in the sitting-room—Maud, Isabel, Mrs. Jackson, and myself—when we heard the front door slam. "It's Sam," said Maud, and she glanced at Isabel, and then both looked at their mother. Mrs. Jackson hastily arose and went out, and presently we heard her gentle tones mingling with some that were rather gruff. Soon we heard footsteps bounding up the stairs, and Mrs. Jackson returned to the room. In a moment the door opened again, and his mother presented "My son Samuel." He was a tall fellow, nearly six feet in height, and with a pair of good honest eyes I noticed at once. He stooped a little in his shoulders, probably the result of too rapid a growth, but instead of walking up to me in a frank, friendly fashion and greeting me as a gentleman should, he shambled across the room and hesitatingly extended a hand whose nails would have been improved by a brushing, and mumbled something by way of a greeting, whose purport I could not understand. After this effort he slouched into a chair and paid no attention to anyone.

When we were called to tea, instead of escorting the guest, Sam lounged along the passage behind us. During tea I took the opportunity to observe him well. His hair was brushed with a wet brush across his forehead, but on the crown an aspiring lock rose most conspicuously; his necktie was crooked, his coat-collar was up in the back, and it looked in need of the brush. It seemed to me very singular that this boy should be so rude when he had a good mother and two nice sisters, genuine ladies all of them. They began to talk with me about Sam a few days after.

"You must not think," said Mrs. Jackson anxiously, "that Sam is really a slovenly boy. He has plenty of baths and clean clothes and all that, but he is so careless in his personal appearance and manners. I talk and talk, but all I say seems to do no good whatever. I think," she added with a sigh, "that if his father had lived he would have been different, for Dr. Jackson was a perfect gentleman, but I don't know how to manage Sam, somehow. He is a good boy," she continued, "he has no bad habits, and he has the best heart in the world. Last winter, when I had that siege with pneumonia he nursed me devotedly, and he is as kind to his sisters as possible. But his careless ways do distress us greatly. I am hoping though," continued the gentle lady, "that as he grows older this bad habit will correct itself."

It seemed to me a great pity that so many fine qualities should be obscured like this, and I thought that probably his mother had been too gentle and indulgent with him and had spoiled him a little. So I resolved that if I had a good opportunity during my visit, I would let him know how his appearance struck other people.

That afternoon I went to the barn with Sam to see Childe Harold, his horse. Childe Harold had belonged to Sam's father, who had been a physician, and at his death he had left the horse to Sam. Of course his mother and the girls drove the horse whenever they chose, but he was Sam's property, and his especial pet and pride.

As we entered the beautiful creature's loose box he came up to us instantly and made my acquaintance in the most gentlemanly manner, smelling daintily of my outstretched ungloved palm, which is always considered a polite acknowledgment of an introduction in the best horse society. Then he accepted a lump of sugar from me and in a moment more his pretty head was pressed against my cheek. Sam was delighted, and so was I. Childe Harold was a beautiful horse, and as he was perfectly groomed from his velvet nose right down to his pretty fetlocks, he was all over as shining and as soft as silk.

"Who takes care of him, Sam?" I asked.

"I do," he answered promptly. "I will not let any one else touch him. I groom him, feed him, and take care of the stable entirely myself."

"He is in beautiful order," said I admiringly.

"He's a regular dandy," laughed Sam, "that's certain. I believe he knows when he is a bit dusty—he always acts kind of shamefaced."

I smiled. "I'm fond of dandies," said I.

"I like a dandy horse," said Sam.

"And I a dandy boy as well," said I.

Sam's lip curled. "I despise them," said he. "Poor dudes! they don't dare do anything for fear they will get their clothes spoiled."

"Don't be too sure of that," said I. "Don't you know what the Duke said about his dandy regiment at Waterloo?"

"No," said Sam.

"He said *they fought well*, and he gave them the hardest post of all on that terrible day, just because he was sure they would not fail him."

Sam stood leaning against Childe Harold's shoulder. He had a little hayseed in his hair and there was a smudge on one cheek, and I resolved to give him a little lecture on the spot.

"I think," said I, "that a boy ought to be not only neat but orderly in his dress, for if his hair is accurately parted and thoroughly brushed, if his coat is put on straight and is well dusted, if he has on a fresh necktie, nice clean linen, and well-blackened shoes, he will respect himself much more than he will if his toilet is only half made; and if he respects himself his manners will be finer and more careful—they will match his clothes. I believe in a boy's paying attention to his looking-glass, and in always dressing just as neatly as possible, for when a boy has the dress and manners of a gentleman it makes every manly quality shine the more. I don't care for diamonds in the rough; I like mine to be artistically cut and polished always."

"I know whom you are aiming at," observed Master Sam calmly; "but I'm not mad, and I will spruce up so tomorrow that you will not know me. How will that suit?"

"Well," said I laughing, "if you will groom yourself as nicely as you do Childe Harold, I will be perfectly satisfied. Surely it is worthwhile to take as much time and pains with the toilet of a boy as one does with the toilet of a horse."

"You are mistaken there," answered Sam. "If I should spend the same amount of time in polishing myself that I do in polishing Childe Harold, I would shine like Grandmother Penfold's silver teapot all over."

"Just you try it and see," was my parting advice as Sam left me at the door.

It is now some years since Sam and I had that talk in the stable, and Sam has learned long since the dress and manners of a gentleman. The most recent event in his history was his marriage, and a few evenings before that ceremony took place, he put on his wedding suit and came downstairs to exhibit himself to his mother and me.

"How do I look?" he inquired complacently, as he drew himself up and squared his fine shoulders in front of us in his immaculate linen, glossy broadcloth, and shining boots.

"Like Grandmother Penfold's silver teapot exactly, shining all over," I answered mischievously.

How Sam laughed! "I remember that talk in the stable perfectly," said he. "It was good advice, and it stuck, luckily for me, for I took it to heart and practiced it. If I hadn't I would never have won Bess, I am sure, for she is the daintiest morsel who ever wore bronze slippers." There came a warm light into his eyes as he bent and kissed his mother's cheek, and then went bounding up the stairs full of joy over the happy days that were coming.

⊰ FOR FURTHER THOUGHT ⊱

1. What does it say about your opinion of others when you keep yourself and your clothes clean and neat? What does it say about you?
2. What does pride in appearance have to do with strong character?

On "Grit"

NEW ENGLAND BOYS HAVE A WORD THEY USE WHEN THEY wish to describe a nature which is absolutely indomitable. It is about the highest praise they can give to a comrade when he puts out the last ounce of his strength in the last spurt which wins the boat-race, or comes out a fraction of a percent ahead of the classmate with whom he has been racing in his Latin or his Algebra all the year. When it is over and the prize is won, his admiring friends crowd around him and slap him on the shoulder and shake him by the hand and say to him cordially, "Tell you what, old fellow, *you've got grit*"; and so he has; and it is this magnificent quality which sooner or later always wins the prize. The grown people call it "indomitable perseverance"; the boys call it *grit*, and I like their word better than the others.

"But," you say, "grit is not everything. A boy has to have a very strong body if he does much at athletics, and he has to have an exceptionally bright mind if he comes out ahead intellectually."

Think a minute. In any trial of strength, who is the most apt to win, the lad who is brimful of pluck and science, who knows just exactly what to do and how to do it, or the big fellow who has twice his muscle and only half as much determination and knowledge? And as for scholarship, every teacher knows that often it is not the most brilliant boy who wins the prize; it is the boy who studies the hardest.

Once I knew a lad who thought he had a divine call to be a minister; he had plenty of good common sense, but he was dull at his books, and some of his friends thought he was making a mistake. They said that Tom would make an excellent farmer or carpenter or blacksmith, but that he was very poor timber to make a minister of. Still, Tom felt that he must try. So he went to college, and one of his tutors, speaking of him, said, "He had the thickest head I ever saw on any boy, and the most difficult to get an idea into; but if once the idea found an entrance, it stayed, it never deserted him, and he was the hardest student that I ever knew." The result was that Tom graduated with honors, for he studied so tremendously hard that he more than made up for the slowness of his mental action, and gradually, as his mind was trained, it acted more rapidly, and he turned out to be by no means a dull young man, and he is now a minister—successful, happy, and beloved by all his congregation.

This quality of grit is well worth cultivating. Everyone who has succeeded in this world has had it; in fact it is the secret of success. Grant had it when the Confederate generals said of him that he did not know when he was beaten. Morse had it when he *would not* give up the electric telegraph, though he should spend every penny he possessed and many long years over it, and his friends should think him a "crack-brained enthusiast." Palissy had it when he burned the very furniture of his home for fuel whereby to feed the furnace which held the precious vessels which he had glazed, and which at last, after uncounted failures, came out perfect from the fire.

Now when this indomitable will becomes a moral force, and is always thrown upon the side of the "Power which makes for righteousness," what a splendid thing it is. The men who do this are the great ones of the earth—the men who help the world forward and make it better, and nobler, and sweeter; for all who come within the radius of their influence are inspired by them and are helped to do their best.

So, my boy who reads this, if you wish to become a noble, helpful man, cultivate this manly trait. Never give up a purpose or an idea if you are sure it is a right one. Never be daunted by any obstacle or disheartened by any defeat. Never mind how many times you fail—keep on till you succeed. Believe in yourself and your own powers and capacities. Be sure that you can be what you wish, and do what you ought, if you only try hard enough. Then when you are a man you will find that things which are very hard, or even perhaps impossible for other men to accomplish, will be easy for you, because you have yourself in such perfect training and under such complete self-control. And people will believe in your capacity and trust your sincerity, and they will be willing to follow your leadership toward any righteous cause which needs brave hearts or willing hands to help it.

≼ For Further Thought ≽

1. What does it mean to have "grit"?
2. The Olympic Games may come the closest to displaying the meaning of grit today. Aside from their physical abilities, what kinds of qualities do the Olympians demonstrate year-in and year-out?
3. What connection does the ability to persevere have with being a success?

What to Do About It

WHEN BERT DROPPED IN TO SEE ME THE OTHER AFTERNOON he looked rather troubled, and after a while he told me what was the matter

"To tell you the truth," said he, "there are things going on in our school that I don't like."

"What is the trouble?" said I. "Tell me about it."

"You know what the academy is supposed to be," he answered. "Any fellow who goes there is supposed to be all right; but somehow this past year or two the tone of the school is lowered. There is a great deal of cheating done in one way or another about lessons. Lots of boys copy each other's examples and exercises, and so on. And that is not all, there is something worse still—they are playing cards for money there every day. Of course if the Doctor knew it there are some boys who would be expelled at once; for they are the ringleaders, and it is they who are at the root of all the mischief. Now, personally," continued Bert, looking me frankly in the face, "I am all right, I'm not in any scrape, you know; but that is not enough for me, for it seems as if I ought to do something to stop this nonsense if I can."

I liked that in Bert, for if we are Christians, it is not enough for us to merely keep ourselves in the right track; it is a Christian's business to help others. So Bert and I began to consider the subject.

"What do you think, Bert," I asked, "since matters have got to such a bad pass, of going to the Doctor and telling him about it? Surely he ought to know."

Bert looked grave. "Oh, yes," said he, "he ought to know; in fact he ought to know that there is something wrong without being told, but he does not seem to." Bert paused awhile; he was thinking. "But I couldn't tell him," he resumed; "no fellow could. It isn't the square thing, you know. If the Doctor asked me about anything, I could not lie out of it, I would tell the truth so far as I knew it; but as for deliberately going to the Doctor and telling him—that would be impossible."

"Well," said I, "I think you are right, Bert. I do not believe in telling, myself, though some very good people do not agree with me on that subject."

"That is because they don't know," said Bert with decision. "If they had 'been there' themselves they would think as we do."

"Well," said I, "could not the senior class be induced to take hold? Are there not enough honorable, right-minded boys among them to cure the mischief? Every time they know of any lying or cheating or card-playing among the younger boys, couldn't they stop it?"

"Yes," Bert answered, "I believe they could, and they could do it without complaining to the Doctor too. They could just take hold and shake it out of those fellows, and nobody could say there was anything mean about that."

"And," said I, "if they found that the matter was too bad for them to cope with unaided, after a thorough investigation and a fair warning they could go to the Doctor in a body and lay the case before him, and he could deal out justice, and dismiss the ringleaders if necessary. You cannot let the academy government go to smash for want of a little plain dealing."

"The bother of it is," said Bert, looking grave again, "I am not a senior, and of course the seniors have nothing to do with us, nor we with them."

"Oh yes," said I, "I know the etiquette. But you are not the only honest boy in your class. Talk to your chum about it and see if he does not wish that things were different. Get as many of your class as you can to say that they wish these bad practices were put down. Get them to sign their names to a paper, so that you may be sure of them, then two or three of you take this paper and go to one of the seniors and lay the case before him. Choose your man carefully, be sure he is an honorable, conscientious fellow, a Christian if possible, and I think he will be willing to help, for the honor of the old academy is dear to most of her sons, I know. If the first senior you speak to will not cooperate with you try another, for there must surely be someone who is willing to start the plan, and the others will join when they find it is for the honor of the school."

"Well," said Bert, as he arose to go, "I believe your plan is worth trying. I will see what I can do. Thank you for telling me."

And to other boys who may read this, and who are in such trouble as Bert was, I will say that I have seen the plan tried, and it has worked with the happiest results. It takes courage to start it, and patience and wisdom to carry it through, yet it does solve one of the knottiest problems that ever confront a schoolboy's life.

◄FOR FURTHER THOUGHT►

1. What's wrong with the popular idea, "Go ahead and do what you want as long as it doesn't hurt anybody"?
2. What does the following saying mean? "The only thing necessary for the triumph of evil is for good men [or good kids] to do nothing" (Edmund Burke). Why is this a dangerous belief?
3. If you saw a friend doing something you knew was wrong, and you had to stop it or at least let someone in authority know about it, what would make the difference between you becoming a tattletale and being a responsible friend?

On Patriotism

ONCE WHEN I WAS VISITING AT WEST POINT I WAS WALKING about the Post with one of the cadets. It was a lovely June day. The air was sweet with the odor of freshly cut grass on the parade-ground, and plenty of soldier boys in their shining white trousers, natty [neat and trim] gray jackets and neat helmets were strolling about, each with a proud mother or sister or cousin at his side. Everybody was happy, for the June examinations were over and everyone had passed safely, even to "Little Texas," who was, I suppose, about as mischievous a lad as ever wore the gray, and yet the pet of the whole Post in spite of his roguery. Even he had been pulled through by the united efforts of his comrades, and came out on the right side of his percentages by the very skin of his teeth, so there was not one cloud on any heart, and everywhere one caught snatches of happy talk and laughter as the merry groups strolled by.

My particular laddie was as happy as the rest, and I was as proud of his six-feet-two of splendid young manhood as anyone could well be. He had been treating me to some of the sort of talk that I enjoy very much from any boy, telling of his life at the Point, describing the very hard study and drill and the rigid discipline which makes the West Point boy the soldierly fellow that he is, and telling too of the various "larks," which the average boy may be relied upon to provide for himself under any circumstances. Thus chatting we chanced to pass the flag, whose beautiful folds rose and fell upon the breeze. My companion raised his helmet as he glanced up at it, and a deeper and more solemn feeling looked for an instant from his honest eyes.

"You do love it," said I, "don't you?"

"Yes," he answered frankly, "next to my mother."

"I wish that every young man in the country loved it as well as that," said I, "but it seems to me that nowadays the average young man knows nothing of such a feeling."

"Nobody says anything about it to them," said Phil thoughtfully; "but we are taught to love the flag from the first minute we reach the Post. I think that makes the difference."

I think Phil is right. The average boy of today is not taught to love his country as he should be. Today patriotism slumbers. If another war should break out it would undoubtedly awake, roused like a sleeping lion, and turn against the foe. But people do not seem to think that the country needs patriotic citizens in time of peace as well as in time of war.

Not long since in a certain ward of a great city which was dominated by the liquor saloon, a few earnest souls endeavored to rouse patriotic citizens to concerted action against this and other evils before the municipal elections. Honest citizens were nominated who would enforce existing laws and institute needed reforms. On election day there were thirty-two thousand less votes cast than there were voters registered. That meant that there were thirty-two thousand men in that ward who did not care enough about a freeman's privilege to take the trouble to cast their votes. It meant also that the powers of evil triumphed once more, for every wicked man in that ward voted solidly for the liquor interest, while the respectable citizens stayed at home resting or perhaps taking little excursions into the surrounding country.

Such facts as these are enough to make even a boy think, and every boy ought to think seriously about such things. He ought to make himself familiar with the history of the United States as it is revealed in the newspapers from day to day. He ought to watch intelligently the legislation not only of the country, but of his own State and town or city as well. He ought to have his views on the tariff, the liquor question, the Sunday question, socialism, monopolies, money, and every other subject which affects the welfare of his country; and then when he is old enough to vote he can exercise that privilege intelligently, and nothing should prevent him from so doing; for surely the least he can do is to cast his vote for truth and righteousness and law and order, and if every conscientious man did that, what a happy country this would be.

This country of ours is, in the eyes of the Old World, merely an experiment still. True it has finished successfully its first century, but what is that fragment of time to the hoary monarchies of Europe and Asia? We have successfully grappled with some giant evils and have slain them, but others are coming on, and whether we will arouse ourselves to meet and conquer them is a question still. It depends upon the boys of today to answer that. It is upon their shoulders that the burden will fall, and they are the ones to whom the fight is coming. Probably they will not have to meet the foe with powder and ball, or to die for the flag amid the din of cannon and veiled in smoke, but it will be no less serious business which they will be engaged in, and it will require no less courage and far more patience, if they are to win the fight.

Therefore, my boys, never glance at the flag without thinking of the meaning which clings to its stars. Never forget what patriots have dared for its sake. Remember that today that flag stands for the symbol of hope and freedom to millions of downtrodden men in the Old World as well as in the New. And finally, resolve never to let it be sullied by any stain of disgrace which you can prevent, while you have a heart that beats in your bosom; and so live throughout your whole life that this dear country of ours shall be better because you have been born an American citizen.

⊰ FOR FURTHER THOUGHT ⊱

1. Why is knowledge of the past valuable?
2. What do the pledge of allegiance and our national anthem, "The Star-Spangled Banner," represent to you? Why does the flag deserve our respect?

On Getting Acquainted
with Christ

I KNOW THERE ARE MANY BOYS WHO WILL READ THIS WHO DO not yet know Christ and who would like to get acquainted with Him; but in spite of all they hear about Him in church, in Sunday school, and prayer meeting, they do not know how to begin; for the things which are said about Him touch upon ideas which are quite outside of their experience and which seem very strange and unreal to them. What is this "still small voice" Christians speak of which brings such happiness to hear? How do Christians know Christ hears them when they pray? How do they know He loves them, and how can they love Him when they have never seen Him? One has to be well-acquainted with Christ before one can understand all this. You will have to be more than an acquaintance, you will have to be a friend of His before you can experience such things. And to become genuine friends with anyone takes time, you know. But fortunately for us, it is very easy to win Christ's friendship, for He is always ready and waiting and we have only to do our part.

The first thing to do is to read the story of His life as we find it in the four Gospels, not reading it piecemeal, a little bit at a time, but reading as if every chapter were a lesson—as indeed it is—and you were bound to get the meaning out of it. When you have done this you will find that there are certain things which Christ expects every friend of His to do. One is to pray—not simply to *say* your prayers, but to pray honestly from the heart. Tell Him that you want to be a friend of His, and ask Him to forgive your sins and make you worthy. You will not hear anything, you will not see anything; when you arise from your knees the world will look the same as usual. Nevertheless, if you have prayed that prayer with an honest heart, it will surely be answered. You will also find, if you want to be friends with Christ, that He expects you to make your life as nearly like His own as you can. To do this there is just one little test which you must apply to your actions every hour in the day—it is to say to yourself, "Would Christ like me to do this?" If you think He would, go on and do it well. But if you think He would not like it, then never do it.

And if you keep on steadily, day by day, reading His Book, praying to Him, and trying to be like Him, then surely some day, sooner or later, you will feel His presence near you, and He will speak to you in that wonderful way of His which one can know but can never describe; and you will be ready from that moment to drop everything and spring with joy to answer when He calls.

Sometimes—I'm sure I don't know how—a boy gets an idea that to become a Christian will take all the fun and sparkle out of life.

"You have to be so awfully solemn," said one of my boys to me once.

"Why, Jack," said I, "what makes you think that?"

"Oh, I don't know," he answered, "but you do."

"Do you suppose," said I, "that when Jesus lived in this world He went about with a sad face and a grave manner and only spoke in solemn tones? No, indeed. If He had been like that, people would not always have been asking Him to dinner and to supper and trying to get Him to stay with them at night. He would not have been a welcome guest at wedding feasts and happy gatherings like that. No. He was cheerful Himself and He loved to have everyone about Him happy, and He was always trying to make them so."

Of any sort of honest, wholesome fun no Christian boy need be afraid to take his share, and he will be apt to have a better time than anyone else, for who will have so light a heart as he? Only take care that no slightest hint of ill-temper or unfairness on your part shall mar any of your games and you can be sure that your Best Friend is glad to have you happy, and that you can serve Him in your play as well as in your work.

And if any boy who does not yet know Jesus will try to get acquainted with Him in the way that I have told, he will soon come to know Him, and when he knows Him he will love Him, and when once he loves Him he will be proud and happy to be His friend and servant until the day he dies.

1. How do you become a Christian? (Read John 3:16, Romans 10:9-10.)
2. How do you know you are a Christian? (Read 1 John 5:1-13.)

On How to Have Fun

At first thought the average boy does not seem to need much instruction on this subject. He takes his fun wherever he can find it, as he goes along, and he rarely misses an opportunity to have a good time by the way. There is sound philosophy in this method of living, and if grown people would practice it oftener than they do they would be the better and happier for it.

There are some boys, however, for whom it would be a good thing if they would stop a little and think about their fun in a reasonable way, because life ought not to be all fun. There are a good many other things that a boy ought to attend to as well as to having a good time. Boys do not always realize that. Sometimes they behave as if their one object in life were to see how much fun they can get into their days. Send them to school, and they slide out of every lesson they possibly can and only learn what they must. Put them to work and they shirk, and will not work honestly and thoroughly, and the spare time which they get in these dishonorable ways they devote to mischief and they call that fun.

The boy who lives on this plan will surely come to grief, and it will be about the deepest grief which can befall a boy. Only those who have been through the experience know how bitter it is. There is an excitement about being the ringleader of your class in roguery at school, I know. The pranks which you play are funny, and you will find plenty of boys who will admire you and cheer you on. But who are your friends in the class? The fine, manly fellows who stand near the head of the class, the ones who know more of the lessons than you do and who can play just as well in the games, the boys whom every one likes and respects, or those foolish, idle lads who keep down near the foot of the class? By and by, when you get "forty marks" and are sent to the Head Master, the glamour will fade away, and your foolish behavior will not seem so amusing.

There is so much fun in the world that is not *good* fun, and sometimes a boy does not discriminate. He takes any fun he can get, and sometimes, alas, he prefers the fun that is not good. Fun that is at the expense of another, fun that teases, fun that is discourteous, cruel, and unkind, is not good fun at all, and it debases the boy who indulges in it; to find amusement in any vulgarity stains a boy's very soul.

I wish boys carried their religion into their fun more than they do. It is an odd thing, but a boy may do honest work, or be a thorough student, and yet not be a right good playfellow. He does not control his temper on the playground and play fairly and pleasantly; he wants more of an advantage than is his due, and sulks if he cannot get it. The way a boy plays and the kind of play he likes best are pretty thorough tests of his character.

There is a good deal of talk in the newspapers just now of the rudeness and brutality of our schoolboys' favorite games, and it is true that a game of football or baseball may be a fine contest of skill and courage and strength or it may degenerate into a savage contest which is a disgrace to civilized young manhood: it depends on the boys themselves. I was watching a well contested game of baseball some time since between one of our large Brooklyn schools and the Freshman team of a neighboring college. The teams were well matched, the scores at that minute stood even, and the excitement ran high, when one of the opposing team, who was running for a base, was hit by the ball. It struck him squarely between the shoulders with a thud that was heard all over the grandstand. Perhaps some of you who read this know just how it hurt. The poor fellow was bewildered for a minute: he threw up his hands and screamed like a girl. In an instant one of his enemies had his arm around him, and before his own friends could reach him our boys helped him on with his jersey and got him to a seat, while our captain ran over with kind inquiries. The trouble was not serious, and presently the lad was up and playing away as hard as ever.

"That was very courteous," I remarked, well pleased, to my escort.

"Why, of course our fellows would be kind," said he, with a little stare of surprise in his blue eyes. "That team are our boys, you know."

But one does not always see such behavior in the field as this, and the only way you can be sure of having it is by keeping the very spirit of Christ in your heart whenever you take your place behind the bat or line up for the struggle in football. If you play as you know Christ would like to have you play, and only like the fun you are sure He would have enjoyed when He was a boy, then your good times will be flawless, and all your comrades will like to be on your side wherever you may be.

⊰ FOR FURTHER THOUGHT ⊱

1. Describe the difference between playing a sport with boys who have to win and those who play for the fun of it.
2. What does the author say is the surefire way to keep the right attitude when you play on a team?

On Minding Your Manners

"I was always taught to be civil,
In the civil old days gone by."
MARY D. BRINE

SEVENTY YEARS AGO, WHEN MY FATHER WAS A LITTLE BOY, HIS
mother's last injunction as he started for school always
was, "Now be sure and mind your manners, my son."
And the little lad, if he met any one upon the road,
whether it was a stranger or a friend, used to draw himself up by the wayside as straight and stiff as a soldier
and take off his cap with a bow; and so did all the other
boys. A boy in those days never sat in the presence of
his elders until he was bidden to do so; he waited until
he was addressed before he joined in the conversation,
and he carefully added the old-fashioned "sir" and
"ma'am" to his "yes" or "no" when he answered a
question. I fancy the boys of today would find such
restrictions rather hard to bear; but the results were
fine, for the manners of the old school were very stately
and beautiful.

Now, though we would not expect any such for-
mal manners from a boy of today, yet it does seem to
me that the modern boy does not always pay quite
enough attention to his elders. He seems to live in a
world of his own. He has his own thoughts, pursuits,
and interests, and it does not occur to him that

grown people would be much interested in them. Yet it would often be greatly to his advantage if he had an older friend in whom he could confide, for the society of those who are older and wiser than ourselves helps to develop us as nothing else can.

When I said something like this to Jack, once, he answered, "Well, I've often thought that I should like to know some grown people better, but they don't give me a chance. Now there's our minister, Dr. Garrison— everyone knows what a splendid man he is. I've often thought I should like to know him well enough to talk to him about things, and I've been introduced to him three or four times, but he doesn't remember me at all; mother has to tell him who I am every time he calls, and he doesn't know me yet on the street."

"But," said I, "when you do meet the doctor you merely say, 'Yes, sir,' and, 'No, sir,' in answer to his questions. You show no more individuality than an oyster; and how can he remember you from time to time? Why don't you talk a little with him sometimes and let him find out what sort of a boy you are?"

"He doesn't care anything about me," objected Jack.

"He would," said I, "if you would let him."

Not long after this the doctor preached a sermon which interested Jack very much and he thought he would like to have it to read by himself, so he plucked up courage to ask the doctor to allow him to take it home with him. "Certainly," said the doctor, beaming upon him from behind his glasses, "certainly, and perhaps you will drop in some day this week and let me know what points attract you most, and if you found any particular difficulties."

Jack, remembering my conversation, did drop in as requested. They began conversation with the sermon for a topic, and then in some way—Jack never knew how—they got around to green flies and red hackle and the best thing for trout in April, and, as Jack afterwards remarked, they got very chummy together. After that Jack had many a good chat with the minister, and a genuine friendship grew up between them which was of great service to the boy.

So, whenever you have the opportunity, I would advise you to cultivate the friends of your father and mother. If, when you come home from school, you find your mother sitting with friends in the parlor, walk in and shake hands and sit down and chat for a little while. Show them a little courtesy as a son of the house, and then you can excuse yourself and go off to your fun with a good conscience. And if you meet friends of your parents when you are away from home, and they do not recognize you, or perhaps do not chance to see you, do not be afraid to walk up to them and introduce yourself. Say simply and modestly, "I am Mrs. Randolph's son Tom, and I know mother will be glad I have met you."

I will tell you a secret: there is nothing an older person appreciates more than such little attentions from the young, and the benefit which they will be to you yourself is beyond telling.

It would not hurt some boys to be a little more courteous than they are to their own fathers and mothers. Surely you should be as quick to help your father on with his overcoat, or to wheel up the easy chair for your mother, as you would be if they were cherished guests.

Sometimes a boy seems to be actually ashamed to try to cultivate a fine manner. He appears to think that the rougher and blunter he is the more manly he will be; but that is a mistake, for it is truly unmanly to be rude or discourteous, and it is well to know *how* to behave on any occasion. An easy manner sets other people at ease. This is where that neat little science called Etiquette comes in. I would advise a boy not to neglect it, for he will find it very convenient to know how to give and how to accept an invitation, when to give a lady his arm, when to offer his hand, and when to bow only. It is pleasant to be able to give an introduction easily, and what a comfort to know so well how to behave at table that you do not have to think about manners at all!

Manners are really the expression of the life. Let me live in the same house with a boy for a week, and notice how he behaves, and I will tell you just what sort of a boy he is. The boy who is kind and pleasant to his father and mother, his brothers and sisters, the guest, the servants, and even to the cat and the dog, is a manly boy.

An English writer, in a beautiful poem, reverently speaks of Christ as "the first of gentlemen," and it is a true and beautiful characterization of Him; and any boy who takes Christ as a model and faithfully tries to be like Him will be sure of having a manner which will never fail him under any circumstances, for courtesy will become a part of his character.

⇥ FOR FURTHER THOUGHT ⇤

1. What is the benefit of having friends who are adults?
2. What does the author say are the character qualities of a "manly boy"?
3. Why are good manners an important part of life?

On Using Your Brain

AMONG ALL MY BOY FRIENDS THE ONE WHO HAS THE KEENEST eye and the cleverest hand is a deaf-mute; and he has also the soul of an artist. "Ear-gate" is closed to him, and all his knowledge must come through the medium of his other senses; and he has made them serve him very well indeed, for he is a more than commonly intelligent boy. In the school where he has been educated he has been taught to talk, and to read conversation as it falls from the lips of others, so that it is quite easy to communicate with him, though his English is sometimes a little odd.

This boy came dashing into our house one Saturday morning; his face was radiant, and he was a good deal out of breath.

"I have found a beautiful thing," he cried. "I have made haste. I have run to come and tell you."

"What is it?" I asked, full of interest.

His eyes were shining with delight. "I have found out how to draw like Nature," he said, and he laughed for pure joy.

"I will show you," he continued. He placed two chairs at the table side by side and thrust me into one of them. Then he wheeled about and took "Webster's Unabridged" from the shelf, and placing it on the table sat down beside me and hastily began to sketch.

In a very few minutes the drawing was done. The angle of the book which was at the greatest distance from him was drawn a little smaller than those which were near, and the proportion was perfectly preserved, a few lines of shading were dashed in, and the little sketch was well-nigh perfect; it stood out from the paper like a solid thing. "See," said he: "that which is farthest is a little smaller than that which is near. When I sketch it so it looks natural. You could pick it up; eh?" He laughed again, then he sprang up and seized another object; this happened to be a whisk-broom; he sketched it, applying the same principle with the same happy result. "So it is with the room," he proclaimed joyously. "So with the house, so with the road, so with all things. I have found it and it is true."

He had discovered and applied the law of perspective entirely unaided by anyone. His friends knew of his love of art and intended that his talent should be cultivated, but it was thought best that his general education should be concluded first, and he acquiesced, but his artistic instinct could not lie dormant. I found upon questioning him that he had been at work upon this problem during his spare hours for many months. "I think and think," said he. "I try and try; at last I find."

I have heard it remarked occasionally—always, I have observed, by those who have not had the advantage of an intimate acquaintance with boys—that "boys are thoughtless creatures." The boys themselves know better than this. The fact is, an average boy thinks more in the course of a day than most people, for a boy is a rapid thinker, and if he has no use for a subject he drops it; so in the course of a day he gets through with a good many ideas. The trouble with a boy's thinking is that he has not yet the wisdom of experience, and so he does not always think to the best advantage. For instance, while it is very good fun, and by no means useless as a mental exercise, for a boy to invent a new language or a new system of shorthand, or to make his own electric battery or run his own telegraph wire, yet he will find it to his advantage in the future if he learns his Algebra lesson first, for really the Algebra is of the greater importance, though it may not seem to be so now. These lessons in school have a practical value, and it is well worth a boy's time to find out what that value is and how to apply it while he has the opportunity.

When I heard the best grammarian of his class calmly use a double negative in ordinary conversation not an hour after he had made his recitation, I felt that he yet had something to learn of the English language. And when the boy in rhetoric announced that he "found a penny walking over the bridge," the statement was more surprising than he realized at the moment, and it showed that he, too, had something still to learn.

The boy who is satisfied when the answers to his examples "come right," though he cannot tell why they are so accommodating, or the boy who can rattle off a rule of grammar as fast as he can say

"Onery, enery, ickery, Ann,
Filisy, folisy, Nicholas John"

and has no more idea of what one means than the other—such boys are not worthy to be called by the noble name of scholar, and it is a pity they cannot resign their opportunities for learning to those who would value them more and use them better.

But a boy uses his brain not only when he is in school but during every hour when he is awake, and since this is the case it is a good plan to acquire the habit of using one's brain always to advantage. You will find life far more interesting if you do that. The habit of observation, for instance, is a most delightful and

valuable one. The various phenomena of nature make
a fascinating study. "Every boy his own scientist," is a
very good motto to take. Notice things, watch them,
see if they occur twice in exactly the same way; find
out, if you can, "why" they occur. Take up a special
subject and follow it out as far as you can.

I knew a boy once who took up the subject of rain.
He measured the rainfall of his section of country for
six months, and his measurements were so accurate
that they came within a very small fraction of being
the same as those of the government. He knew the
length of time of every rainfall during that six
months, and of course how many inches of water fell
each time. He knew from what point of the compass
each storm came, and whether the wind changed during the rain; he knew which were the most destruc-
tive and which were the most beneficial storms. He
read up on storm centers, and the little book in which
he had garnered his statistics was very interesting
reading, while he had acquired much information
which was really valuable.

I knew another boy who went into the country for
the summer brimful of curiosity about all sorts of
things, and one day he brought into the house a pail
full of water wherein a great number of what country
boys call "wigglers" were disporting themselves. He
thought that they were tadpoles, and he expected
much pleasure from watching their transformation
into frogs. They did not seem to grow very fast,

however, while each morning their number became less and less and his room fuller and fuller of mosquitoes, fine lusty fellows with good appetites; but the problem of Jack was, What became of his tadpoles? Did they eat each other, or what? He hung over the pail for hours; at last he caught one of the sly little creatures in the very act of changing, not only his place of residence, but his very form of life, and then what a burst of wrath and astonishment overcame this young observer! He got an old lace veil of his mother's and tied it over the pail, and then he had them; and what that boy did not know about mosquitoes in the course of a few weeks was not worth knowing. He got his tadpoles later.

Then there is the habit of reading; an excellent habit, truly, if you read good books and remember and think about what you read. The best book in the world will be quite powerless to help you if you do not read it rightly.

Now is your training time; now you are learning how to become master of every power that you possess; and if you are careless of your opportunities now you will be less of a man some day than you might have been. But if you are like my brave Ethred, of whom I told you in the beginning of this chapter, "to think and think, and to try and try," you will find just when you most need it that you have the lever of Archimedes in your hand; you will be able to move things to some purpose.

⊰FOR FURTHER THOUGHT⊱

1. Why was the boy at the beginning of the story so excited about being able to draw?
2. Sometimes we think we're smart when we know a bunch of facts. How is "using your brain" different from just knowing facts? Give some examples of how this kind of knowledge can help you throughout life.

Your Own Opinion

THE SUBJECT OF THIS TALK WAS SUGGESTED BY A LITTLE CHAT which Jack had with his mother the other day. He had been telling her of something that had occurred during the midwinter examinations, which were just past. Jack had given his next neighbor three dates for his History paper.

"But, Jack," said his mother, "was that honorable?"

"Why, mother," answered Jack, "all the fellows do it."

"That's not the point," she said gently; "do you think it was right?"

"Harry would have thought I was awfully mean if I hadn't."

"Would you have accepted such help?"

Jack wiggled a little. "Well," he admitted, "Harry

did give me one little hint in my Algebra. Turn about is fair play."

"Of course," said his mother, "Professor Simpson knew all about it."

"Of course he didn't!" returned Jack a little impatiently. "Mother, you don't understand. All's fair in love and war, and this is war. The professors are on one side and we are on the other. They know how it is. If they catch us, all right; but if we can beat them, why, we come out ahead."

"And do all the boys in your class act on that principle?"

"Yes," answered Jack, "I suppose they do; at least I don't know any one who does not."

"Now, Jack," said his mother, looking at him seriously, "I want you to forget about the other boys and their ideas, and I don't want you to think whether you like or dislike your masters; but, judging by the standard which the Bible gives, I want you to tell me whether you think you have acted honestly."

Jack was silent for a minute and then he said slowly, "Well, no."

Some time since I was talking with a young man who was in business in New York, and he told me this story. He was in the wholesale nail trade, and the price of nails was so low that the nail dealers were losing largely; it was decided that something must be done, and all the merchants agreed not to sell nails below a certain reasonable price, and were free to get as much

more than that as they could. The head of the firm
with which my young friend was connected entered
into the combination but gave private instructions to
his clerks to sell all the nails they could at a trifle less
than the price agreed upon. The consequence was that
while the other firms held to the agreement faithfully,
this man for some weeks sold more nails than any
other dealer in New York, and he made a deal of
money.

"But," said I to the young man who told me this
narrative, and who laughed at the sharp practice, "do
you think that was right?"

"Well," he answered uneasily, "of course it was not
right in the abstract, but Mr. B— made a lot of money,
and one expects double-dealing in business; it is an
understood thing. A man can't make money without it."

"Do you know what you are saying?" said I. "You
are saying that there is no firm in New York which is
prospering that is making money honestly."

"Oh, I don't mean that," said he, roused at last,
"but it is a fact that there are lots of deceits practiced
in business."

"And you," said I, "were beginning to think that
perhaps it did not matter so much after all!"

I once spent about two years in a town where
nearly all the young men were in the habit of playing
games of chance for money. I was talking to one of
them about it.

"Oh," said he lightly, "all the fellows do it. I would look odd if I didn't."

"But do you think it is right?"

"It is my own money that I lose."

"Whose is it that you win? You get something for nothing then, don't you? Is that honest? You know that some of the young men in this town have been ruined by betting and gambling; perhaps you have helped to do it by playing with them; at any rate, you have had the experience of playing games for money. You know the excitement of it and the temptation of it. Now, honestly, looking at it from all sides, do you think it is right?"

He was an honest boy at heart; he flushed, but he looked me in the eyes. "No," said he, "I don't."

It is much the easier way for a boy to think as the other boys think, to accept their standard of morals and to do as they do; but a boy will surely come to grief if he allows himself to drift like that.

The only way in which you can become a strong and noble man is for you to think over every question of morals for yourself, being quite uninfluenced by popular ideas, and never giving a decisive regard to any considerations of your own pleasure or profit; and then, when you have formed your own opinion, abide by it, careless of what anyone may say. Take the Bible for your standard, be governed by your conscience, enlightened by that divine word kindly given to be a light to our path, and you will never go far wrong, though you may sometimes find yourself standing with only the best of your young associates around you. But never mind that. Better stand for the right with Christ by your side than to be wrong with the whole world for company.

⊰ FOR FURTHER THOUGHT ⊱

1. Have you ever defended something you shouldn't have done by saying, "Everyone else does it!" What's wrong with using that as an excuse?
2. How could you become a person people call strong and noble?

On Being a Christian

WHEN A BOY GETS ONE GOOD LOOK AT THE SAVIOR, AND REALIZES something of what He is and what He has done for us, it is not often that that boy turns away and leaves Him; for after such a look one can hardly help loving Christ and trying to serve Him. But sometimes a boy's idea of what constitutes a Christian life is not very clear.

I asked one of my boys once how anyone could tell whether a boy was a Christian or not.

"Well," answered Tom rather hesitatingly, "if a fellow is a Christian, he goes to church and to Sunday school and to prayer meeting regularly, and he reads his Bible and all that."

"But," said I, "I am sorry to say that I have known some people who have done all those things you mention and yet I did not feel sure they were true Christians. Is there no other way in which you can tell? How do you know that Will Barrett is a Christian, for instance?"

"Why," said Tom at once, "*by the way he acts*. He isn't the same fellow at all."

"Ah," I responded with a smile, "now you have explained it perfectly; *he isn't the same fellow at all*."

It is not any one thing that a boy does, but a change occurs which penetrates his whole life. That is what we mean when we say anyone has been "converted," or has had a "change of heart." It is what the Bible means when it speaks of being "born again," or of "becoming a new man in Christ Jesus." The change is radical, and a boy who has been through that experience is not the same fellow at all that he was before it happened. It is not only that he takes a deeper interest in his church and all its services than he ever did before, or that he reads his Bible more faithfully or prays more earnestly, but the change affects every action of his daily life; it makes more thorough the way he works or studies or plays; it makes him braver, gentler, pleasanter than he ever was before. But the change is shown most of all in the way he fights and conquers his own besetting sins. And when a boy's companions see such a change as this coming over one of their number they know beyond all doubting that he has become a Christian, and such is the test which a boy's friends always apply to him.

Once, not many years ago, a boy went to college, and he was just the handsomest, wittiest, pleasantest, and most "taking" boy in his class. He had plenty of money, everybody liked him, and he was sought after by all; but he made friends with the faster and more reckless set, and for two years he went dashing on, and there was nothing too mad or too foolish for Jack Sanborn and his friends to do. But in one vice he was worse than all the rest: he was exceedingly profane. The habit grew upon him until he swore without knowing it, and it was second nature to him.

One day he chanced to be sitting in his room alone when someone came to him. He never could tell how it was, but it seemed to him that Christ was there—the Christ of Calvary. He had heard the Bible read thousands of times, indeed, he had been taught to read it and to pray when he was a little boy; but it had all been to him as an idle tale. But in that hour Christ came to him and called him, and he heard and answered, and forsook all and followed Jesus as truly as did those fisherman friends of Jesus so long ago by the Sea of Galilee.

His comrades noticed the change in him, of course, and they watched him, half-laughingly, half-curiously, but very closely. He was just as friendly as ever with them, but to their wonder not one glass of wine would he touch, not one bit of dissipation would he indulge in, and strangest of all, not one profane word passed his lips. For the rest he was much as usual—better at his lessons a good deal, but happier and more full of life than ever. He was deeply interested in the inter-collegiate games, and he was highly excited over a certain coming football match which, according as it was won or lost, would be the glory or despair of the collegiate year.

"I will tell you what, fellows!" said one of his friends, "if Sanborn gets through this football match without swearing I shall think his change of heart is a genuine thing."

When the decisive day came Jack drove a party of friends to the game.

"It will be a dry lunch, fellows," said he when he invited them. "Nothing but Apollinaris water."

But his friends knew very well that there would be a delicious luncheon provided, and one who voiced the sentiments of all remarked that he "would rather go with Jack Sanborn and Apollinaris water than with any other fellow and champagne." So they all accepted the invitation, and then every one agreed to watch closely and see if sometime during the day Jack did not forget himself and swear. But Jack never dreamed that he was under such a close surveillance.

The game was an exciting one, and Jack and hundreds of others like him screamed and shouted and cheered their favorites on. The excitement became constantly more intense. The team of Jack's college was losing ground. Jack was half beside himself as he stood upon the seat. Suddenly there was a suspicion of foul play on the other side, and that roused Jack's blood to fever heat. His lips opened with a hoarse cry, but no words came. He clenched his teeth just in time. His shut fists plunged into his coat pockets, a great vein swelled out on his forehead, and he sat suddenly down, gazing straight ahead, never seeing that struggling heap in the field which a minute before had held his whole attention, for he realized that he had very nearly disgraced his Lord and Master. There was one instant's prayer, an unspoken thought, and he was self-controlled once more and turned his attention to the game again. He never knew that his struggle was noticed, but every one of his companions had seen it, and they knew better than anyone else could know what an effort it was for Jack to so control himself.

Not long after this there was a revival in that college, and it began among Jack Sanborn's set. The old president—a saintly man—was filled with wonder, and called it a "marvelous providence," as indeed it was. Jack himself never knew that he had anything to do with it, but it is true that the sight of that noble resistance of his to sharp temptation convinced all who saw it of the reality of his religion, and made them long to know for themselves this Master whom he served so truly; and so in the most natural way the beautiful influence spread, until more than a hundred young men sought that Savior whom Jack had found and promised to love and serve forever.

And so, my boys who are Christians, never, *never* forget that it is by the common acts of your daily life that you are going to be judged; it is by them that you will stand or fall; it is by them that you will influence others; and it is the smallest things sometimes that are the most significant.

I think that one of the best texts for a Christian boy to guide his life by was given by the apostle Paul; for he was a man who understood boy-nature very well, and boys just growing into manhood were always very near his heart.

This is the text I speak of, and I will leave it with you, making it the closing sentence of my book:

"Therefore, whether ye eat or drink, or whatsoever ye do, do all to the glory of God."

⊰ FOR FURTHER THOUGHT ⊱

1. What happens to you when you become a Christian? What does the phrase "change of heart" mean?
2. Why is it important to watch what you say and do in front of others? When no one is looking?

There's more to teaching your kids about sex than a nervous discussion of the birds and the bees.

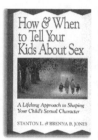

Our children are inundated with messages about sex. Everywhere they turn—in our neighborhoods, school, and the media—they are bombarded with discussions, jokes, debate, and mixed messages about sex. So how can we make our input count?

Stan and Brenna Jones suggest that sex education is not so much about information as it is about character formation. How our children act when it comes to sex isn't a matter of information, Bible verses, or warnings. It's about who they are.

How & When to Tell Your Kids About Sex will help you move beyond the "sweaty hands" approach to telling your kids about sex and give you the tools you need for building Christian character in your children that will equip them to take a stand and make the right choices.

How & When to Tell Your Kids About Sex: A Lifelong Approach to Shaping Your Child's Sexual Character (Stanton L. & Brenna B. Jones) 0-89109-751-1/$18

Available at your local bookstore or call (800) 366-7788 to order.

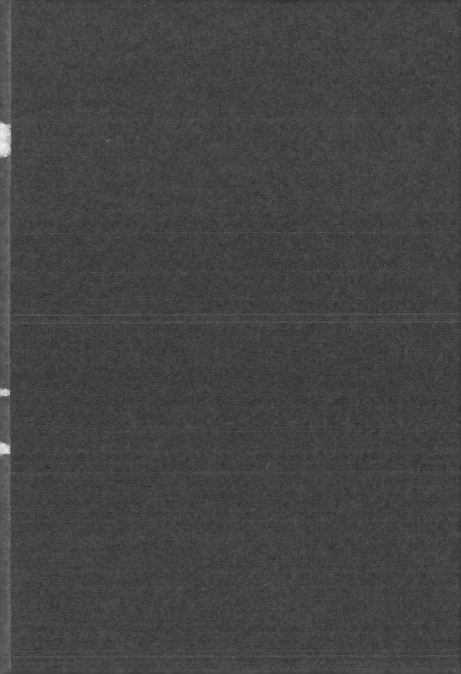